Praise for the Book

"101 Things To Do Before You Graduate is essentially your college experience syllabus. Just as you receive and use a syllabus at the beginning of a class to map out how to successfully complete the class, you should use this book to accomplish the same goal for your overall college experience."
Steve Loflin, Founder & Executive Director of the National Society of Collegiate Scholars

"If you want to build a solid foundation for an inspired life, you must read 101 Things To Do Before You Graduate and then do them. It will pay off in ways you can't even imagine."
Andy Chan, Vice President of Career Development at Wake Forest

"Jullien and Patricia's 101 Things is more than just a list. It's a way to challenge yourself, embrace your potential, and discover new opportunities. I wish I had this book my freshman year."
Allen Gannett, Co-Founder of CampusSplash.com

"College students have so much potential, but often not the direction and guidance to unleash it. Patricia and Jullien's book provides that guidance yet allows college students to choose their own paths to success."
Nicole Lindsay, Executive Director of New York Needs You

*"The **101 Things** list sets college students up for success by offering a comprehensive guide to being a well-developed contributor to society. Life as an undergraduate can be especially ambiguous and confusing if one does not have a path to pursue. I believe that guidelines found in this list can be highly beneficial to a student looking to either establish or enhance their net potential—and all before they graduate!"*
Mary Snowden, Assistant Director of Multi-Cultural Career Programming at New York University

*"Teaching 1000's of students each year I realize how blessed I am and more importantly, that the future will shape up very well. Part of that "shaping up" will come from students who see the academic experience as a life experience – that is the beauty of **101 Things To Do Before You Graduate**."*
Keith GeLarden Dayton, Senior faculty lecturer and MBA Core coordinator at Indiana University Kelley School of Business

"We check off things to accomplish in our everyday lives, but how often do we make a list that will impact our long-term career development? Patricia and Jullien have pulled together a simple guide to help college students get to the next level as they prepare for their careers after graduation."
Rosalie Schraut, Associate Director of the Career Prep Program at Management Leadership for Tomorrow

*"Brilliant!!! **101 Things To Do Before You Graduate** is like a bible for self-actualization through college."*
Jemima Fortune, Coordinator of Student Leadership at North Georgia College & State University

"The 101 Things list is a great guide for college students' skill development. It's everything we have tried to tell our own kids put in its most simple form. At College Unbound—our new innovative college—we are using these 101 Things as a guide. I would take The 101 Things list over a lot of other things we expect students to do in college."
Dennis Littky, Co-Founder & Co-Director of Big Picture Learning and The MET Center in Providence

"This to-do list for college students highlights the importance of diversifying skill sets, taking risks, being proactive, and excelling academically. Having worked with young adults for over 10 years, I value the innovative and stimulating approach that this book takes regarding the pursuit of one's dreams."
Joyce Cadesca, Director of Alumni Program at the Beginning with Children Foundation

"Education is all about learning how to learn, learning how to go beyond opinions, and looking at evidence to make informed decisions. By taking the driver's seat and following the 101 Things To Do Before You Graduate, you can significantly accelerate your learning and earn the training you need to keep learning. This guide will help you keep yourself accountable on your long post-graduation road to personal and professional significance."
Mrim Boutla, Founder & Chief Career Officer of PurposeU.com

101
THINGS
TO DO
BEFORE YOU
GRADUATE

PATRICIA HUDAK & JULLIEN GORDON

ISBN 978-0-9844518-4-5
Published by: Real World 101 Media & The Department of Motivated Vehicles
www.101Grads.com

www.101Grads.com

101 Grads Speaking

THANK
YOU
DEEPLY...

Acknowledgments

Patricia's

As is the case with any major accomplishment, it is never done by just one person. Therefore, there are many people to acknowledge for their help in creating this book. If any were not mentioned, please do not feel as though you were forgotten—I appreciate you.

A BIG thank you to Jullien for his tireless work and commitment to the vision of the book. It is a pleasure working with you and I look forward to what we can accomplish in the future together.

To Annetta Hanna and Tanya Arditi, thank you both for your excellent work editing the book.

To Arel Moodie, thank you for your encouragement, motivation, and enormous energy.

To Sheena Lindahl, thank you for always being there for me and being the best friend anyone could have.

To Bert Gervais, thank you for teaching me the value of great mentors.

Thank you to all of my friends and acquaintances who gave feedback on designs, reviewed the book, sent me encouraging emails, or simply asked how my company was doing. Your simple gestures helped make my dream come true and for that I'm extremely grateful.

ACKNOWLEDGEMENTS

To my family, thank you for supporting me and keeping the dream alive.

To my parents, thank you for allowing me to follow my crazy dream while carrying some of my financial burdens. Your encouragement means more to me than you can ever imagine.

Finally, thank YOU, the reader, for reading this book. Now go make a better future for yourselves and our entire generation.

Jullien's

To The National Society of Collegiate Scholars for your trust, belief, and investment in me to start this movement in 2010 with the N.S.C.S. Route 66 Tour and your continued support of my growth and development along with that of a half million other N.S.C.S. members nationwide.

To all of the 101 Grads out there who are actively taking control of their lives, checking off their *101 Things To Do Before You Graduate* list, and seeking to maximize college by developing their personal, intellectual, social, and financial capital before graduation.

To the UCLA Community Programs Office where I grew exponentially as an undergraduate because of the safe and fertile space it created for me to complete this list before it manifested as this book.

To Joey, Hung, and Teddy for being great examples of what 101 Grads do by taking the initiative to create the 101 Grads iPhone application to spread this message nationwide through students' mobile phones.

Table Of Contents

MONEY   127

Manage Your Money

Make Money

TABLE OF CONTENTS

Personal Growth

Foreword

I always remind high school and college students that college is a fresh start. A new beginning. A clean slate.

College is a wonderful and unique opportunity to create, invent, reinvent, experience and challenge yourself in ways that can take your life in a plethora of new and unexpected directions. A chance to explore, experiment, try new things and repurpose your life.

When you get to college you will be filled with a true sense of possibilities. You will have this clean canvas and you alone will be the artist to paint and create your college experience. You will choose your major, choose your classes, choose your friends, and maybe most importantly, choose how to spend each and every hour that will become your college experience masterpiece.

Too many students start with so much ambition and then allow every day to become a routine. The time goes by very quickly and the degree is earned, but the possibilities are not truly explored and the potentially life-changing experiences are missed.

With that in mind, Patricia and Jullien have created a valuable tool and must-have resource for every aspiring and current college student. *101 **Things To Do Before You Graduate*** is brilliant.

This book is essentially your college experience syllabus. Just as you receive and use a syllabus at the beginning of a class to map out how to successfully complete the class, you should use this book to accomplish the same goal for your overall college experience.

I highly recommend this book. It is a tremendous and easy-to-follow resource that will help you explore, get you out of your comfort zone, allow you to create, think and learn while overall pushing you toward making your college experience a fulfilling, regret-free educational experience.

Remember, it is *your* college experience and it will only be great if you choose to work hard and if you choose to make it great. Start reading the book now and start checking things off the list, and truly start embracing and maximizing the incredible potential of college.

Stephen E. Loflin
CEO & Founder
The National Society of Collegiate Scholars
Washington, DC
www.NSCS.org

Introduction

You are awesome for even opening this book. It communicates that you know there is more to college than just classes. You know there is more to life. You know there is more to you. Hopefully we can help you maximize your college experience, your life, and your potential.

Today, even a 4.0 GPA isn't enough to guarantee your success after college if your college isn't preparing you for the real world. The world has changed significantly over the last few years due to the internet and globalization, and will continue to change at an ever-faster rate. How will you keep up if your vehicle for success—your college education—is going too slow?

Will you graduate with an expensive piece of paper or with practical tools to use in an uncertain future? When you divide your annual tuition by the actual time you spend on campus in class and doing extracurricular activities, you are likely paying almost $1 per minute for your college education. How are you making use of that money?

Most college graduates expect a *return on their investment*, but the reality is that many college graduates are *returning home* after graduation because college has failed to teach them how to navigate change, create value for others, and handle the real world. On the other hand, college never promised you that it would do those things. It promises to provide you with the tools and the space to prepare for success in life, but you have to pick up the tools and use them.

Many of us only went to college because we knew we were *supposed* to. When we ask college students why they are in college, most don't have a legitimate answer other than that. Instead of thinking of your college education as just four more years of forced schooling, there's an alternative, and far more rewarding, way to view this experience.

Since birth, you have lived on other people's schedules and you've been measured by grades. In kindergarten you hopped on the assembly line of education and rode it all of the way through high school. College is your first opportunity to take control of your education, your future, and your own destiny because for the most part, you get to choose how you spend your time and what you're going to learn.

Think of college as four years of time and space to create your D.R.E.A.M. life. The way we define D.R.E.A.M. is your **Desired Relationships Employment And Money**. College used to be the best route to a good job—but not necessarily a D.R.E.A.M. job. And college used to be a pit stop on the way to living the American D.R.E.A.M., but this no longer holds true.

Although a high GPA is touted as the Holy Grail in education, it doesn't measure how successfully you've actually learned a subject. Instead, it measures your ability to follow the rules. The world's most successful people don't follow the rules or embrace society's definition of success. We each have our own definition of success, but in general, success is the ability to be who you want to be and do what you want to do when you want to do it. A college degree doesn't guarantee you that kind of success nor, in fact, does the highest-paying job in the world if it sucks your happiness and energy.

The 4.0 that really matters in college is the degree to which you develop your 4 capitals—personal capital, intellectual capital, social capital, and financial capital. A student who focuses on these four things will be more likely to succeed in life than someone with just good grades. We want you to have book smarts and street smarts.

Personal capital has to do with **how well you know yourself**. How clear is your sense of purpose? What are your strengths and passions? What motivates you? What are your weaknesses? What is internally stopping you from becoming who you want to be and doing what you want to do? Do you have an entrepreneurial mindset or a mindset of entitlement? Your answers to these questions reflect how well you know yourself.

Intellectual capital is all about **what you know**. Four years of focusing on your major will help you acquire knowledge, but how comfortable would you feel lecturing about your major for an hour or more upon graduation? Since there are probably hundreds of students with the same major at your school alone, what other subjects would you be ready to tackle on a game of Jeopardy? What skills do you have that set you apart from the average person? Your intellectual capital may have nothing to do with your college major. Perhaps your school doesn't offer courses in the subject you know best or are most passionate about, but that doesn't mean that you can't use your four years to develop an expertise.

Social capital is **who you know and who knows you**: it is your network up, down, and across. Most of us are great at networking across, within our own peer group. If you flip through the contacts in your cell phone, 95% of your contacts will likely be people in your peer group who are within 3-5 years of your age. Networking with peers is great, but since they are in the same boat as you, they can't always expose you to new opportunities and information or open doors that you want to get into. College is a great opportunity to build your network up with your access to alumni, professors, staff, and upperclassmen. Later on, your network will also stretch down to include people who work for you or learn from you.

Networking up is ten times more powerful than networking across or down, because someone above you on the totem pole of life generally has more power, more relationships, and more wisdom to help you along your journey. And don't forget that networking up should include aunts, uncles, your parents' friends, mentors, and community members. Networking down includes engaging with mentees, underclassmen, and siblings who can also support with manpower, fresh ideas, and contacts.

Financial capital is a tricky one—it results from a combination of your intellectual and social capital. Your financial capital will be based on **who knows that you know what you know**. The reason we get paid to speak at colleges across the country is because the right faculty, staff, and students at universities nationwide (our social capital) know that we know a lot about maximizing college (our intellectual capital) and when those two things intersect, financial opportunities start to flow. You can be at the top of your class in your major, but if the right employers don't know that you are an expert in that field, job offers will not flow your way.

In building a solid foundation to your life, start with your personal capital. See what interests arise out of you truly knowing who you are. Start acquiring intellectual capital in those areas of interest. From there, your social capital will develop among people who share your interests and passions. And finally, financial opportunities will begin to flow in the form of internships, jobs, entrepreneurial opportunities, and positions that affect the flow of financial capital (e.g. student government, programming committee, etc).

We want to help you use your campus' intellectual, social, and financial capital to develop yours so that you graduate with far more resources and opportunities than you had when you entered as a freshman. Your campus' intellectual capital includes your professors, classmates, guest speakers, libraries, online databases, courses, departments, and centers. Its social capital includes alumni, student groups, programs, and events. And its financial capital includes student government, scholarships, grants, financial aid, the career center, and equipment that you have access to that non-students would have to buy or rent.

At the end of the day your college major should be yourself. Though you will master different subjects during college, understanding who you are is the number one thing you can learn. Unfortunately, there won't be many classes offered that will allow you to discover who you are. You will spend your time learning about Einstein, Hemingway, Roosevelt, and other prominent people in history and you can apply their insights to your life. But *you* are the most important thing you can learn about and the degree to which you master this subject will determine much in your life. This book offers you *101 Things* you can do to get to know yourself over the course of your college experience. Let's get going!

How To Use This Book

This book is designed to be a quick read so that you can spend more time taking action and checking off your list than reading.

For each item in the list, we explain why the action is important, how to get started, and then offer you resources (i.e. websites, products, or services) that will help you complete the action. The book is organized into four keys areas—academic, career, money, and success—so that you can focus your efforts on specific areas you want to grow in.

You can use the Table of Contents as your master checklist and/or you can check off each item by chapter. And the great news is that you probably already have momentum because you've already completed a few things on the list! Flip through the Table of Contents, check those items off, and then get started on the rest.

We suggest that you choose 12 to 15 items to focus on at the start of each semester. Beginning with the end in mind will help you establish a vision and action plan for your *traditional education* of classes, papers, and exams and your *non-traditional education* of the **101 Things**.

As an additional resource, on **www.101Grads.com** you will find:

1. **Inspiration**: College students' stories about their experiences as they work on their own checklists. Feel free to share your story as well to inspire others.

2. **Insights**: Advice and answers to questions and challenges you and others are facing with college and your transition into the real world.

3. **Innovation**: New items or ideas that we and our readers thought were cool that weren't in the original *101 Things*.

4. **Information**: Additional products and services that we and our partners offer that may help you complete a particular item.

If you like what you read and experience with the *101 Things*, we would love to come to your campus and speak. Typical events include orientations, student success or career classes, conferences, and academic excellence workshops. Give us a call at (646) 875-8477 if you're interested, or visit us at **101Grads.com/Speaking.**

Academic

A college degree used to be the best way to get educated *and* get a good job, but a degree no longer guarantees either of those goals. Education is changing, the workplace is changing, and the world is changing. Success will increasingly come to the person who knows how to ask the right questions and creates new knowledge based on insights gained through inspired inquiry.

Intuition, not tuition, will be the future of education. In Latin, to educate literally means to draw out. This implies that intelligence and knowledge are already inside of you and that great educational institutions and great teachers create environments that allow you to discover the answers already within you. Unfortunately the educational system—K through

12 and college—isn't evolving as fast as the world you're going to graduate into and is therefore ill-equipped to offer you the optimal environment to discover tomorrow's knowledge.

The best way to explain this is by using the analogy of the tortoise and the hare with a twist. In this version, the hare thought to itself, "In order to win the race with as little effort as possible, I'm going to jump on the back of the tortoise and relax there. Once we get close to the finish line, I'll jump off and be well on my way to success."

Sounds easy, right? Well, the hare is you and the tortoise is your education. Here you are, this fast-thinking millennial who can multi-task with a computer, phone, and music while writing a 30-page paper, sitting on top of an educational system that hasn't evolved nearly as fast as the world it was designed to serve. We want to get you off the tortoise so that you can start learning at your own pace.

We've been taught to take the path of the hare or the hypotenuse of higher education—class to dorm, dorm to class, class to dorm—and that this will ensure our long-term success. We've been taught that the direct line is the best line, the safest line, the shortest line. It's not true. In fact, the road less traveled is the best way to get to your D.R.E.A.M. faster, more securely, and more easily. ***The way to maximize any experience is to do more than is expected of you***. Now is the time to take risks. Face your fears. Take the road less traveled.

Since we're talking about your college experience, the road begins with academics. But signing up for more classes and taking more tests is not the solution. How many times have you fallen asleep or skipped a class? How many times have you crammed for an exam and forgotten everything the moment you exited the exam room? You have to admit that there are cheaper ways to learn much of what is on your course syllabi. For $30 a month you could get an internet subscription and you would have access to 80% of what a student paying $30,000 a year in tuition has at your school.

What you've bought with that money is not a bunch of classes —you've bought time to educate yourself. When you look at college as time you've bought, your big question should be: How am I going to invest this time? A lot of students waste time, take their time, give their time, lose time, try to save time, spend time, run out of time, and do everything but invest their time. If you sleep in until 2pm on Saturdays, you may have had fun on Friday night, but you're probably not getting the most out of college or life. Instead, you could be actively seeking experiences that are going to give you resources to draw upon later when the stakes are higher and the choices are tougher.

Start by evaluating your academic path. You may be majoring in a subject that you don't like or stuck in a program that doesn't align with your career interests and goals. If you know this, begin to figure out how to change direction. On the other hand, if you love your major, consider how to maximize its value. Or you may still be up in the air about what you want to major in. In any of these cases, the items in this section will help you discover who you want to be. As you check off the items on the Academic list, you will develop the courage you need to choose, accelerate, or change your academic program.

☐ 1. Complete Your Academic Plan

Going to college is one of the biggest investments you'll ever make in your life—it's usually more costly than a car and often more expensive than many houses. Not only are you paying a large sum of money to attend, but the return on making the right investment can be much greater than you can imagine. However, people often spend more time deciding how many rooms they need in a house or the color of their car than they spend planning out their college classes.

Every minute you spend planning out your time in college increases your likelihood of graduating on time or earlier. With a plan in mind, you will be able to not only take the required courses, but have the opportunity to take graduate level courses **(SEE #21)**, write a thesis, or study abroad **(SEE #6)**. Your academic plan involves laying out your classes by semester to make sure you're taking the right pre-requisites so that you can get into your major and graduate on time. It's a simple process, but oftentimes it is overlooked.

Getting Started:

1. Write down your academic goals, such as date of graduation, major(s), minor(s), GPA, and academic accomplishments in a Word document or a journal.

2. Meet with your academic advisor **(SEE #2)**.

3. Find out the credit requirements for graduation and for your major(s) or minor(s).

4. Ask your advisor the typical academic path of a student who wants to achieve the goals you've listed.

5. Create a document that lists what courses you would like to take each semester from freshman to senior year.

6. Mark required courses with a star.

7. Write the number of credits for each course.

8. Total them all up to see if you meet graduation and degree requirements.

9. Review your plan with your academic advisor and a mentor.

❐ 2. Meet With Your Advisor 3 Times A Year

Your academic advisor should be your B.F.F. (best friend forever) in college. Turn to him or her for real help. Think of them as your personal guide to help you navigate the system. The primary duties of academic advisors include:

1. Assisting students in developing educational plans that are consistent with their life goals.

2. Providing students with accurate information about academic progression and degree requirements.

3. Helping students assess campus resources that will enhance their ability to be academically successful and overcome educational and personal problems.

If your school assigns you an academic advisor, this doesn't mean that he or she is your only option. If you are not satisfied with the help provided by your assigned advisor, ask if you can change advisors. Other students know which academic advisors will give you the best advice and assistance. Ask around and be sure to ask more than one person.

An alternative is to consider speaking with another advisor, while continuing to use the assigned advisor to process your paperwork.

Getting Started:

1. Find out who your academic advisor is.

2. Set up an initial meeting with your advisor to create your four-year plan.

3. Be honest with your advisor about your plans and what kind of course load you can handle.

4. After the meeting, schedule two more meetings with your advisor to update him or her about your progress.

5. Talk to your advisor often about how your semester is progressing. Doing so will increase their willingness to write letters of recommendation and help you in times of need.

❒ 3. Go To Office Hours

Do not be intimidated by your professors. They choose to teach. They want to help you. They want to share their passion with you. Ask them questions. Allow them to get to know you. If they don't approach you, then you must approach them. In college, you need to be the one to reach out to your professors. Start by going to them during their posted office hours.

The benefits of taking advantage of a professor's office hours are endless:

- Your professor will know you by name and you will establish a relationship that will last beyond the class and semester;

- You will get inside information about what to focus on for the upcoming tests or assignments;

- You get the benefit of the doubt if your grade is ever on the border line.

You will be surprised by how few people attend office hours. The one-on-one attention you get may be all you need to finally understand a major concept or overcome a problem with an assignment. In some cases, office hours are actually more valuable than class time.

Getting Started:

1. Before going to office hours, make sure you've done the work and have regularly attended class.

2. Let your professor know if you don't understand something in class. Usually, you're not the only one who missed what was being taught.

3. Go to class review sessions.

4. Talk to professors one-on-one to see if you can get some direction on what to study.

5. Put in the effort and take the advice that your professor gives you.

6. Integrate office hours into your weekly schedule, especially before major assignments or tests to stay on track and get help.

❑ 4. Meet The Department Head Of Your Major

Learning about your college major involves more than just meeting degree requirements. Employers look for students who not only have taken classes, but who have experience and in-depth knowledge of their field. An excellent way to begin your immersion into your major is by meeting the department head of your major.

The department head knows not only the ins and outs of your industry, but also which professors and classes you should take to make the most of your time on campus. Each department has different opportunities for students, including scholarships, internships, assistantships, events, and job opportunities. These opportunities are easy to miss if you're not aware of what's happening in your major's department.

Don't be intimidated by titles. And don't stop with just the head of the department. Talk to the graduate students and other professors in the department as well. Take advantage of being an eager college student and meet anyone who is willing meet you.

Getting Started:

1. Go to your major's department.

2. Set up an appointment to meet with the department head.

3. Talk with the department head about your future plans and ask for any advice he or she can offer.

4. Attend events organized by the department.

5. Keep the department head up to date with your progress by emailing them each semester about how you are doing and the successes you've achieved.

❐ 5. Take A Professor To Lunch

Your relationship with your professors is not the same as it was in high school with your teachers. Most college professors want you to see them as mentors instead of as authority figures who have to manage classrooms and give grades. They want you to join their team, in a sense. In spite of this, most people graduate from college without any relationships with their professors.

Professors are great to add to your network. Professors serve as links back to your campus and its resources after you graduate. They not only help you learn more about your major, but can introduce you to people in the industry that can hire you.

In addition, you will most likely need a letter of recommendation **(SEE #53)** for graduate school, a fellowship, or a job in the near or distant future. If a professor knows you by name (as opposed to student ID number), they can write one for you that will have the most impact.

Find a professor whose research you are deeply interested in and invite them to lunch. Professors eat too!

Getting Started:

1. Look at the directory of professors and find out what they are researching.

2. Visit the professor during their office hours and personally invite him or her to lunch with a clear reason why.

3. Prepare for the lunch by finding out more about the professor and making a list of questions you want to ask.

4. Make the lunch about them by focusing on their research and their career path. Find out more about his or her experiences and ask for advice they may have for you and your career.

NOTE: The most budget-friendly way to do this is to invite them to the school cafeteria. When you're there, be courteous and offer to pay by asking, "Can I get you anything?" while in line. Most likely they will choose to pay for themselves.

❐ 6. Study Abroad

As the world becomes more and more interconnected, and globalization expands, having an international perspective will give you a huge advantage in life and your career.

Employers like the look of time spent abroad -- travel really does broaden and mature the traveler, and it shows some initiative and resourcefulness on your part. Plus, you'll be practicing languages where they're spoken -- you'll have to use that high school Spanish, enabling you to raise the level of your proficiency on an employment application. Since most Americans don't travel abroad, you could conceivably have a leg up when it's time to travel for business. ("Send Jamie to Thailand for the merger -- she's been there before...").

It's important to get your passport and see how other people live throughout the world so that you can learn to appreciate different cultures and question some of your own habits.

Getting Started:

1. Go to the study abroad department on campus. Find out what programs and countries are available to you and the requirements.

2. Check out **StudyAbroad.com** for opportunities. There are many study abroad programs run by other schools and organizations that you can participate in and receive college credit for.

3. Calculate the cost of studying abroad by creating a budget for travel, living expenses, and college courses.

4. Apply for study abroad programs and scholarships offered by your school as well as other colleges and organizations.

5. Get a passport even if you aren't financially able to travel. It's always good to be prepared for any international travel opportunities that may come your way.

❐ 7. Ask A Question In Class

How many times have you sat in class feeling lost and confused? You look around you to make sure you are not alone and everyone is mumbling and tapping their neighbor on the shoulder because they are just as lost as you. Either you dozed off, the professor skipped 3 steps because they've been doing this for decades, or you missed a key concept in last night's readings.

This is your chance to be a hero and be humble. On one hand, you get the chance to ask the question that everyone wants answered, but nobody else is willing to ask. On the other hand, by asking you have to be vulnerable and essentially admit that you're lost and confused. Ultimately, you help everyone. You help the professor become a better teacher. You help your classmates catch up. And you help yourself in an area of uncertainty.

The ability to accept that you don't understand something and then having the courage to ask someone who does—especially publicly—will get you to your desired destination in life faster than pretending you know everything. Use this as an opportunity to overcome your fear of not knowing.

Getting Started:

1. Attend class and be attentive.

2. When a question arises within you—no matter how simple it may seem—ask. You're likely not the only one with that exact same question.

3. Also feel free to bring up a question related to your readings or a specific problem or concept from your homework.

4. Follow up with the professor after class to say thank you or ask for more clarity.

❐ 8. Learn A Foreign Language

We live in a globalized world where more and more people speak multiple languages. English is only the fourth most spoken language in the world; it is behind Mandarin Chinese, Hindi, and Spanish. As the world gets smaller and smaller, communication will be an increasingly valuable skill. When it comes to communicating ideas cross-culturally, knowing another language will also help you understand other cultures on a deeper level, since language serves as the building blocks of culture.

Speaking a second language is important for professional and personal reasons. Professionally, it can easily distinguish you from another job applicant or from a co-worker when it's time for a promotion. If a company wants to expand to a Spanish-speaking country and you know Spanish, guess what? You're going to be at the top of their list as the person who can do the job. Personally, learning a new language presents a new challenge that has a clear effort-and-results curve and will stimulate your mind in new ways.

Many colleges have a foreign language requirement. Whether yours does or doesn't, we highly recommend that you take a language course and take it seriously with the intention of ultimately being able to speak conversationally—not just to pass the class.

Getting Started:

1. If your school requires you to take a foreign language, find out who the best teacher is and immerse yourself in the language. Find interesting websites, films, music, even restaurants that originate from the country whose language you are learning.

2. Even if your school doesn't have a foreign language requirement and you're high on self-discipline, visit **RosettaStone.com** for software or **Openculture.com/ FreeLanguageLessons** for free online courses.

3. If you need more discipline and structure to stay on track, search for classes off-campus.

4. Befriend a native speaker or fellow classmate so that you have someone to speak to and practice with regularly. This will increase your retention of the language.

☐ 9. Take A Random Class

In college, your education can be on your own terms. Although most majors have degree requirements, there is room for you to pick and choose what you want to study. You're spending a lot of money on your education, so why not make the most of your investment?

Take an elective class that has nothing to do with your major. Choose something that you've always been vaguely interested in but never had the time or resources to explore. Don't take them just because you think they'll be easy, though. One elective can become the class that changes the course of your life.

Getting Started:

1. Make a list of 10 things you've always wanted to learn more about.

2. Read through the course listings to see if your interests are available as classes or to see what classes are available that pique your interest.

3. Ask around to find out what fun classes other students have taken as an elective and see what they recommend.

4. If you have a good academic advisor **(SEE #2)** they can point you toward classes that may not be well known around campus.

❐ 10. Conduct Research With A Professor

Research is a fundamental skill for effective problem-solving and when done right, it will garner insights about a particular problem or question that can be used to create value for the world. Doing research is an opportunity to deepen your understanding of a subject and gain new skills, as well as deepen a relationship with a professor whose work you admire.

The lessons you learn from this experience will set you apart in your academic and professional career. You will be able to articulate insights about your field of study or work that go beyond textbooks and tests, and you will be able to demonstrate the critical thinking processes that helped you arrive at your new conclusion.

Other benefits include the opportunity to get published **(SEE #12)**, or potentially start a company if the discovery is big enough **(SEE #66)**. Your professor will also know you well enough to write a quality letter of recommendation **(SEE #53)** for graduate school or your next job.

Getting Started:

1. Identify a professor whose research you respect. This can
    be one of your current or past professors, or someone in
    another field.

2. Read a few of their writings to gain clarity on why they are
    doing this research, what they've discovered so far, what
    they hope to find in the future, and why this finding would
    be significant.

3. Draft a hard-copy letter and/or email demonstrating your
    interest in the professor and their work. Conclude with a
    request to meet in person to discuss joining the project as
    a paid or unpaid research assistant.

4. In the face-to-face meeting or a follow-up email, explain
    why you care so much, what you hope to contribute, and
    what you hope to gain from the experience.

☐ 11. Finish An Assignment A Week Early

Almost all of our lives have been dictated by someone else's schedule and timeline. From birth to kindergarten your parents ran your life, but as soon as you entered school, teachers determined what you did during the day and after school with homework. Though parents may be out of the equation, your teachers have matured into professors and now they shape your college experience.

This is your opportunity to find or create a challenge that you are so passionate about and immersed in that you complete it on your own timeline instead of your professor's. Whether it's a paper, project, or presentation, challenge yourself to do great work instead of just doing it for the grade. Great work goes beyond grades — it's work that you are proud of, regardless of the grade you may receive.

If the academic rigor of your classes isn't really challenging you all that much, you have to find ways to challenge yourself if you want to be great. When you create a challenge for yourself that matches your skill level, you may experience flow. Flow is a mental state similar to what athletes call "being in the zone." It is characterized by high concentration, a distorted sense of time, and intrinsic satisfaction. Ideally you would cultivate this experience with everything you do, but for now we're just encouraging you to go for it once by finding or creating an assignment that truly inspires you.

Getting Started:

1. In a class that you are interested in, identify a paper, project, or presentation that you want to go above and beyond on.

2. Set your own timeline and checkpoints with your TA or professor to complete the assignment one week before the due date.

3. Widen the scope of the assignment to test your full knowledge and skills and clarify why this assignment is important to you personally.

4. Get started. Don't procrastinate because remember: You are doing this for yourself.

5. Watch the look on your professor's face when you turn it in one week early and then watch the grade you get when they have a week to grade just your assignment.

☐ 12. Get Published

In college you're going to write countless papers, but very few of them will be read by more than your TA, and maybe your professor. We're sure there are some good ideas and points in that 30-page paper somewhere—or did you make up stuff just to meet the page requirement?

Figure out what you have to say that's original or interesting or valuable and then get it published. This doesn't mean you have to be the next J.K. Rowling or Malcolm Gladwell. There are many ways to publish your work in college. You can write for the campus newspaper in the opinions section sharing your side on a current debate. You can write articles for the college or town magazines, and there are countless websites seeking content. You can publish an article with a professor that you've done research with **(SEE #10)**. Or better yet, you can publish a book, like us.

Being published somewhere other than on your own blog adds credibility to your ideas, thoughts, and writing. It's the difference between a book saying "National Best Seller" on the cover and one that doesn't. Being published by a credible journal, newspaper, magazine, website or publisher is a huge achievement and validates your contribution to whatever subject you choose to write about.

Getting Started:

1. Identify which form of publishing will be most valuable to you going forward. If you plan to stay in academia, you may want to publish in a professional journal. If you want to go into business, you may seek to get published in a newspaper, magazine, or on a prominent website. There are print and online outlets for every area of interest.

2. Write a powerful piece for the media outlet you choose.

3. Promote it widely to people in your social network who you think will be interested in what you have to say.

4. If you're interested in publishing a book, check out **101Grads.com/Self-Publish**.

❒ 13. Apply For At Least 1 Scholarship

Most students do not pay full tuition, and you shouldn't either. A great way to get money for college is through scholarships— they're not just for incoming freshmen.

There are scholarships for all kinds of unique things if you search hard enough (there's even one for left-handed students). Going through the application process is valuable in itself whether you get any money or not. Writing an essay that could get you $10,000 is just as easy as writing all those other essays you've been assigned. When else are you going to have the opportunity to make that much money in such a short period of time?

Don't give up your scholarship search when you step foot on campus. There's still plenty of scholarship money out there for freshmen, sophomores, juniors, and even seniors. You are at an automatic advantage if you continue to search throughout your college career because most students give up too soon.

If you are having trouble getting scholarships, there's still hope. When you get your aid package each year, contact the financial aid office and make sure you're getting the best deal.

Getting Started:

1. Visit your financial aid office to find out if there are any scholarships, grants, or additional funding that can help relieve your debt burden.

2. Join campus clubs, fraternities/sororities, honor societies, and other student organizations. Many offer scholarships to members *and* non-members.

3. Join national organizations such as the Rotary, Kiwanis, or Moose Lodge, which offer scholarships to members or the children of members.

4. Search online for college scholarships. Don't just search by major—also search by profession, ethnicity, religion, gender, age, state, etc.

5. Ask the department head of your major **(SEE #4)** if there are any internal school scholarships available to students in your major or school of study.

❏ 14. Graduate 10 Times More Prepared

Though this list will prepare you for the real world in ways your classes won't, you should still graduate. Whereas many of your classmates will be returning home, you will be getting a return on your investment. When you graduate your parents will be extremely proud of you, but most importantly you will be proud of yourself knowing that you got the most out of college and are prepared to get the most out of life.

The items you have completed in this first section of the *101 Things* will help you develop your academic excellence and prepare you for success personally, professionally, and financially. And we honestly believe that if you complete as many things of the *101 Things* as you possibly can, you will be 10 times more prepared for the real world than those who graduate alongside of you.

The real value of your college education isn't in your diploma, it's in the experiences you choose and create with the *101 Things* list and beyond. Many people will graduate with an expensive piece of paper. Only a few will graduate with priceless experiences that will help them successfully navigate the real world. The *101 Things* will help you develop your street smarts, but you still need to get your book smarts.

Getting Started:

1. Create an academic plan **(SEE #1)** for your time at college.

2. Visit your academic advisor **(SEE #2)** during your junior year to lay out an academic plan that will ensure that you graduate with the right credits in the right areas.

3. Complete as many things on our *101 Things* as you possibly can.

4. Graduate on time.

☐ 15. Participate In A Campus Tradition

Every college has its own unique history and with that comes a set of unique traditions.

If you took a campus tour when deciding to attend your college or during freshman orientation, then you may have heard some of the stories and traditions that have been passed down from generation to generation of students.

There are the popular and well-known traditions like the freshman class yell at midnight the night before exam week begins, or the senior stroll down College Ave. There are also traditions that aren't talked about on campus tours, but that are kept alive and spread by students.

It's easy to dismiss traditions as cheesy or corny, but that's for people who don't want to have fun and participate in their school's history.

Getting Started:

1. Go on a campus tour **(SEE #17)** to find out the traditions your college promotes.

2. Ask around and find out about more traditions from students, especially those in upper classes.

3. Involve your friends when participating in a tradition.

4. Create your own tradition with friends.

☐ 16. Lead A Campus Organization

Leadership is the number one currency in today's marketplace. Showing leadership experience and potential is more important to your future than your GPA, major, minor, or school name. College is a great time to develop your leadership skills because there are so many leadership opportunities in student government, student groups, fraternities/sororities, intramural sports, and more.

Membership in a student organization is not enough. The gap between membership and leadership is huge—there is no comparison. Significant leadership in two organizations that you care about is more powerful than membership in five prominent on-campus organizations. Leadership isn't about acquiring a position or title—it's about moving an organization or group of people forward and leaving the organization in a better place than you inherited it.

The beautiful thing about being a leader in college is that the responsibility is high, but the stakes are extremely low if you fail. The alternative is to be placed in a leadership position later on where a mistake can impact the lives of many employees. Test your leadership skills and learn the hard lessons now when it's safe to make mistakes. You have the passion, power, and people to lead a local, national, or global movement right where you are. If you care about something enough, why not try?

Getting Started:

1. Check out **101Grads.com/Leadership** to read an article on Level 5 Leadership and expand your understanding of what it means to be a great leader.

2. Search your school's website for on-campus student groups and clubs and find one or two that interest you.

3. Also check out **StandNow.org**, **FreeHugsCampaign.org**, **EnergyActionCoalition.org**, and other movements started by young people just like you for great ideas and examples of student leaders.

☐ 17. Take A Campus Tour

Wait, what?

You may think you know the ins and outs of your campus, but we bet there have been times when you've found yourself saying, "I didn't know that was there." Within a few weeks anywhere, we develop set routines. We go to this building and that building, and then we go home. As a result, we miss out on everything our campuses really have to offer.

A campus tour will help you familiarize yourself with your campus again, learn something you didn't know, find out more about campus traditions **(SEE #15)**, or even find a faster way to class.

Your campus offers a multitude of resources and opportunities. By not knowing what is available to you as a student, you aren't maximizing all of that tuition you are paying.

Getting Started:

1. Go to your campus' welcome/information center.

2. Sign up for a tour.

3. Bring a friend along for added fun.

4. If you are touring with high schools seniors, share your positive experiences and stories with them.

5. If tours are not available, try to pick up some information at the center and stroll around parts of campus you are not familiar with.

6. Take time to stop inside different departments and introduce yourself.

7. Be sure to visit your alumni office, career services office, financial aid office, student life office, major department, etc.

❏ 18. Attend A Guest Lecture

Colleges are great for bringing to campus people who are leaders in their fields, whether it's scientists, writers, politicians, or entrepreneurs. It's one of the rare places where you can learn directly from the experts and meet them face-to-face. After you graduate, you'll likely have to pay a pretty penny to even get a chance to see these experts. You've probably heard of Jeff Bezos (Founder & CEO of Amazon.com) visiting Princeton, or Steve Jobs (Founder & CEO of Apple) and Oprah Winfrey (Founder & CEO of OWN) at Stanford, and all of the campaign trail stops President Barack Obama made at college campuses. Those are just some of the once-in-a-lifetime experiences you are privy to as a college student.

By attending a lecture you not only receive amazing insights, but you can also receive extra credit from your professors. If you mention to your professor that you are planning to attend, he or she may offer you some extra credit in exchange for a paper written about your experience or the topic discussed.

Getting Started:

1. Look around campus on bulletin boards, newspapers, newsletters, listservs, and online for lectures and events happening on campus.

2. Talk to your professors to find out what lectures you should attend.

3. Ask your professor if there is any extra credit that can be garnered from attending a lecture.

4. Go to the lecture alone so you will be forced to talk to people and network with other attendees.

5. After the presentation, there is usually a question and answer period. Try to be the first person to ask a question. The presenter will very much appreciate you asking that question and will be more willing to connect with you after the lecture.

❐ 19. Join Your Alumni Association

Alumni associations are ready-made networking opportunities where you can connect with professionals who share your alma mater. These networks offer professional development opportunities, mentors, casual and formal networking, and exposure to various career paths.

Too often, undergrads think that alumni associations can only help them after they walk across the stage and receive their diploma—that's not true. Alumni associations have many ways to help you build your network and make the most of your time on campus.

Building relationships with alumni is one of the most valuable things you can do during college to prepare you for life after college. They have the keys to the doors you will be knocking on. They are less receptive after you graduate, so take advantage now!

Getting Started:

1. Visit the alumni office.

2. Ask them about programs they have specifically for undergrads and how you can get involved before you graduate.

3. Volunteer to help in the alumni office.

4. Sign up for alumni newsletters and mailings.

5. Sign up for access to the alumni database.

6. Attend alumni events and meet alumni face-to-face.

7. Donate to your alumni association. It doesn't have to be a large amount—anything you can give is appreciated.

❒ 20. Take The GMAT, GRE, LSAT, Or MCAT

In the same way that you took the SAT during your junior year of high school, you should take your graduate school exams during your junior year of college, even if you're not sure you want to go to graduate school yet. Doing so gives you the option to apply to graduate school if and when the time is right for you.

It's best to study for the exams when you're in an academic environment. Most graduate school exam scores last up to five years, so you might as well take the exam while you're in student mode rather than try to study while working 40+ hours per week. Prepare for this test as seriously as you would any other test. It will have a larger impact on your life than any test you take for college credit. If you don't have the self-discipline, hire a tutor, take a prep class, or find a study buddy.

If you are leaning towards going to a professional school like medical school, law school, or business school, there are specific tests you must take for admissions. If you're unsure of what you want to do next, just take the GRE for now. You may get the score you need the first time around. This will then allow you to focus on the subjective parts of your graduate school applications, such as your purpose statement.

And that's where the true benefit lies in getting the exams out of the way early in the application process. Having the time to focus on how you present yourself gives you the opportunity to differentiate yourself from other applicants. Hundreds of other applicants will have your exact same test score, but nobody can have your unique essays.

Getting Started:

1. Visit **101Grads.com/Grad-Exams** for basic information about the various graduate school exams available.

2. Sign up to take the appropriate test at **ETS.org**.

3. Check out the various test preparation companies such as **Kaplan.com**, **PrincetonReview.com**, or **TestMasters.com** and find the one that fits your study patterns and budget best.

4. Study! Study! Study!

❒ 21. Take A Graduate School Course

As an undergraduate student, you are not limited to taking only undergraduate courses. If your college or university offers graduate programs, you have the opportunity to sit in on a class or two.

Graduate classes are an excellent way to get a deeper understanding of your field. Taking a graduate level course as an undergrad shows mentors, potential employers, and graduate schools your commitment to your continuing development.

Graduate school and undergrad are a lot different. Before committing to graduate school and more debt, sit in on a graduate school course to see if you like it.

Getting Started:

1. Check out USA Today's Best Graduate Schools Rankings at **101Grads.com/Best-Grad-Schools**.

2. Schedule a meeting with your academic advisor to talk about what graduate level courses are available for you to take.

3. Find out if there are any requirements you need to fulfill before you can take a graduate course.

4. Talk to the professor of the course to see if he or she can help you get approval for the course.

❐ 22. Visit A Graduate School

One of the biggest decisions you'll need to make before you graduate is whether or not to go to graduate school.

Please keep in mind: Graduate school should not be your default option.

Sure, the real world is scary, but eventually you are going to have to face it. Getting a higher degree because you can't find a job isn't always the best solution to a tough labor marketplace. There should be more to going to graduate school than a desire to avoid the real world. There is no guarantee that the economy will improve while you are in graduate school, so delaying the real world could leave you with more education and more debt without improving your job prospects.

Don't take your decision to go to graduate school lightly. Treat it the same way you did deciding where to go to college, but with this being a more expensive decision.

Getting Started:

1. Talk to your advisor about what graduate school degree would be right for your career goals.

2. Check out USA Today's Best Graduate Schools Rankings at **101Grads.com/Best-Grad-Schools**.

3. Approach the admissions office of the graduate program at your campus that interests you and ask to do a classroom visit. They will schedule you to sit in on a class so that you can experience the difference between graduate school and undergrad.

4. Take a graduate school course **(SEE #21)**.

5. Register for graduate school exams if necessary **(SEE #20)**.

COLLEGE IS A 4 YEAR STEPPING STONE FOR YOUR 40 YEAR CAREER

Career

College used to be the best route to a job but in 2010, only 25% of college graduates graduated with a job. The unemployment rate for millennials is around 18.5%. That's higher than any other group in the country, including your grandparents. A college degree has become the equivalent of a high school diploma in many respects. Though a bachelor's degree from even the most prestigious university doesn't guarantee a graduate a good job, college is still a valuable time to position yourself for your career path.

In fact, the transition from your academic career to your professional career is the greatest career change that you make in your entire life—unless you go on to become a professor. For the last 16 years, your job has been to be a student but once you graduate, you suddenly have to prove to potential employers that you can do more than write papers, read books, and go to class. The rigorous interview process will force you to demonstrate that you can create real value in the real world and that you embody characteristics like leadership, initiative, and a good work ethic.

On your résumé, your GPA only says so much. It will be no more than four characters placed in the upper right-hand corner of your one-page résumé. What matters more is what fills up the rest of the résumé including your work experiences (e.g. summer jobs and internships), your leadership experiences, your honors and awards, and your skills. Most of these things will come from how you spend your time outside of the classroom.

The number one issue that college students hear when trying to get their first job out of college is: "You don't have enough experience." And then the confused student asks, "How do I get work if I need work experience to get work?" We call this the work experience trap. The only way out of it is to do real work—not just homework—during your undergraduate experience. Whether your real work comes from an on-campus job or an internship, or from leading a student organization, real work will teach you what homework can't. It means dealing with real-life problems rather than problem sets. It means showing up daily, not just when something is due. Real work is all about dealing with the unpredictable.

Up until this point, you've always known what is next. After elementary school comes junior high school. After junior high school comes high school. And after high school comes college. Life is easier when you know what's next because you don't have to deal with uncertainty. In most cases, your college major won't track directly to a career path. The only majors that really do so are in the sciences and engineering. At the end of the day, your major probably won't matter that much.

If you don't have a ready answer when your parents, relatives, or friends ask, "So what are you going to do with that major?" you may be tempted to grab at any career with a definite path. Many people choose their careers primarily to avoid uncertainty, treating their decision like a multiple choice test:

A. Teacher

B. Doctor

C. Lawyer

D. Engineer

In a survey taken of 3,891 American adolescents, 10% wanted to be doctors, 7% lawyers, 7% teachers, and 5% engineers. The only problem is that these professions don't make up 29% of the economy combined. These percentages are more than 10 times the number of actual doctors, lawyers, teachers, and engineers there are.

The primary reason students choose these paths isn't because they are passionate about kids, health, justice, or how things work—they choose these traditional paths because they are safe and certain. If I choose to be a doctor, I know that after college I have to take the MCAT and go to medical school. I know what my life is going to look like for the next 10 years and I can guess at my salary thereafter.

But what about option "E. Other" on the multiple choice test? When you take out all of the outside influences—your parents and peers, the media, the need to make money, what you think you already know about how the world works—and start from scratch, what can you discover about yourself? Start with your passion, not the profession. Start with yourself, not your peers or parents. Start your career in college.

You may think that you already know what you want and what you don't want in a career. After all, you've been exposed to any number of jobs through the media. Doesn't a career as a designer mean creating fashions for the runway? Yes and no. When you properly research career paths, you will find that your sense of the paths you can actually pursue is probably very limited. So use college to explore as many career paths as possible in order to make an informed decision. If you land on teacher, doctor, lawyer, or engineer after doing a thorough inner-search and research, then that's fine. But don't cross out other areas of interest right off the bat.

Your career choice is perhaps the biggest decision you will make in your entire life since you will spend more time in your career than with your family and life partner. The following chapter will help you to explore your options and prepare for your entry into the job market. You can use college as a four-year stepping stone and training ground to create the 40-year career and life you want. And the earlier you invest your time into your desired career path, the greater the return will be in your life.

"BE THE CHANGE YOU

WANT TO SEE IN COLLEGE"

- REMIX OF MAHATMA GANDHI

❐ 23. Perfect Your 30-Second Pitch

Meeting people can be awkward, especially when you're first entering any kind of professional environment. You need to prepare a quick way to introduce yourself, no matter where you are or whom you're meeting. This will help you put your best foot forward in any situation and then see where the conversation goes.

Perhaps the best way to open up any professional conversation after exchanging names, talking about the weather and the latest sports scores, is with a 30-second pitch. Your 30-second pitch is a condensed version of your bio. It explains who you are, what you do, why you're here, and what you're hoping to achieve. The purpose is to give the other person valuable information about yourself in the case you may be of service to them or they may be of service to you. As you mention your school, major, employer, hometown, or passion, perhaps something you say may connect with them allowing the conversations and relationships to develop.

In reality, nobody just starts talking for 30 seconds about themselves. The key ingredients of your 30-second pitch will come in the natural flow of the conversation. It's great to start off with a 5-second pitch that includes your name and something unique about you that sparks the listener's curiosity such as "My name is Jullien and I'm a PurposeFinder." Once their interest is piqued, you will have the opportunity to share more of who you are. Hopefully you'll get to know who they are in the same way.

Getting Started:

1. In 5 sentences, answer the questions "Who are you? What do you? Why are you here? Where you're trying to go?"

2. Rehearse your responses to the bathroom mirror or on a personal web cam until your delivery is fluid and confident.

3. The next time you meet a professional, attempt to use your 30-second pitch and see how it goes.

4. Continue to rehearse and revise your 30 second pitch until you feel entirely comfortable delivering it.

☐ 24. Build A Personal Board Of Directors

Why do PhD candidates have advisor teams, top executives have boards of directors, athletes have fitness coaches, and presidents have cabinets? Because no one person can know or do everything, but the collective wisdom of a team of people with different strengths can fill the gaps.

In *Who's Got Your Back* by Keith Ferrazzi, Keith talks about creating a support team that will help you not only achieve your goals, but also become a better person through accountability. This is not one of your run-of-the-mill group project teams that's randomly put together. Instead, it's a small group of people whom you can trust and who will provide you with encouragement, support, honesty, and guidance.

Your personal board of directors should be a group of people who can serve different roles in your life. *Vital Friends* by Tom Rath identifies a few roles you should consider—Builder, Companion, Connector, Collaborator, Energizer, Mind Opener, Navigator, and Champion. People who can fill these roles include parents, friends, family members, mentors, professors, significant others, and advisors. You should be able to call on these people when you have specific needs that their strengths can support.

Getting Started:

1. List the roles identified in *Vital Friends* and identify two or three people who can fill each role for you.

2. Craft your vision, list some of your goals related to that vision, and state your roadblocks.

3. Send individual invitations to the people who fit the different roles. In your invitation be sure to give specific reasons why you chose them to be on your personal board of directors.

4. Share your vision and goals with these people. Open up a conversation about how your goals align with their strengths and their capacity to support you on an ongoing basis. Chances are they'll feel pleased to be invited to play a meaningful role in your life and will be inclined to help you.

5. Schedule regular calls or in-person meetings with those who accept your invitation to keep them up to date on your progress and challenges. This brings in the sense of accountability: in return for their support, you're committing yourself to moving forward.

6. Find *Who's Got Your Back* by Keith Ferrazzi at **101Grads.com/Whos-Got-Your-Back** and *Vital Friends* by Tom Rath at **101Grads.com/Vital-Friends**.

❒ 25. Contact 3 Successful Alumni

Colleges give you more than just a diploma; they give you access to all of their alumni. We already encouraged you to join the alumni association **(SEE #19)**, but now it's time to take action and leverage your membership.

Who wants access to a college's alumni? You should!

Your school's alumni are perhaps your most valuable resource for exploring career options. If you ever wanted an easy way to quickly build your network in a particular field, your college's alumni database is a great place to start. As a student you already have something in common with your alumni—you both went to the same school. However, once you graduate, they are less receptive to answering your calls or emails.

Most alumni are willing to share their stories, advice, and experience with students. Alumni associations and career services departments provide you with multiple opportunities to interact and connect with alumni, so there's no excuse.

Alumni won't come to you, you must go to them. Offer to take them out for coffee or lunch.

Getting Started:

1. Go to the alumni office.

2. Ask if they have an alumni mentorship program. If so, sign up!

3. Ask if they know of any successful alumni who are working in careers you are interested in.

4. Request an introduction or contact information.

5. Get access to your alumni database.

6. Select 3 successful alumni you would like to meet.

7. Send them an email to introduce yourself and invite them to lunch. For an email template to send out, visit **101Grads.com/Alumni-Email**.

8. Attend alumni events and continue to meet active alumni.

❏ 26. Get A Mentor

Later on we will discuss being a mentor **(SEE #83)** but first you should find a mentor who can help you get where you want to go. Being mentored can help you achieve your goals faster, learn from other people's mistakes, and get introductions to people and resources that you wouldn't have known about otherwise.

A mentor is usually a go-to adult that you can call on at any time. There are many aspects of your life and you may need someone to guide you spiritually, mentally, physically, professionally, academically, socially, romantically, or financially. In most cases one person can't fill every role, so that's why we encourage you to build a personal board of directors **(SEE #24)**.

Some people say they have a mentor, but when you ask them when they last met or talked, they can't remember. That's not mentorship—that's an acquaintance. A true mentor is someone that you check-in with on a regular basis to make sure you're going in the right direction. They are committed to your growth and development without necessarily telling you how or where to grow. Engage your mentor by scheduling monthly calls or meetings. Keep them updated on your progress. Take them out for coffee, lunch, or dinner. Invest in them the way they invest in you and you are guaranteed to get returns on your relationships.

Getting Started:

1. Search your school's website for mentor programs for students and if possible, submit an application.

2. Consider the adults in your life whom you respect. Cultivate a relationship with at least 1 that is willing to invest time, energy, relationships, and resources in you.

3. Schedule your first meeting, develop questions you'd like to ask them, and follow up after the meeting with your notes, action items, and a thank-you note **(SEE #81)**.

❏ 27. Join A National Association Or Organization

At this point in your life you have one or two homes—your hometown where you grew up and your college town, unless they are the same place. As a result, you probably have networks in the community you grew up in and in the community you're developing on campus. Both communities offer you social capital that will be valuable to you in your future. But what if you could expand your network nationally or even internationally?

There is a 50-50 chance that you will not stay in your hometown or college town forever. One way to increase your mobility after college is to develop your national network now. Many honor societies, fraternities/sororities, as well as professional, religious, and cultural organizations, have national networks. By joining the campus organization, you automatically become part of the national organization.

It's one thing to be member of a campus-based organization, but joining a national organization will expand your network greatly. This multiplies even more if you take on a leadership role and participate in annual conferences and regional summits. We encourage leadership because membership isn't enough. Membership has its benefits, but leadership is where the real opportunities to learn, travel, and grow are.

Getting Started:

1. Research the student groups on your campus and consider joining an honors society like the National Society of Collegiate Scholars (**NSCS.org**), a fraternity or sorority, a pre-professional or business-related organization such as the Association of Certified Public Accountants (**AICPA.org**) or Students In Free Enterprise (**SIFE.org**), or a cultural organization like The National Society of Hispanic MBAs (**NSHMBA.org**).

2. If there are none, you can research national organizations that you want to be a part of and see if they have processes to establish student or campus chapters. You can then become a chartering member at your school.

3. Make sure you invest time in national events like conferences, summits, and trainings so that you can meet people from all over the country that share your interests.

☐ 28. Attend An Industry-Related Meetup

The first thing you probably picture when someone mentions a networking event is a group of people standing around wearing name tags and shaking sweaty hands.

Well, not all networking events are like that. A networking event can be something formal like an event held on campus with potential employers or it can be as informal as a guest speaker event or a party.

The key to finding a good networking event is to start with one on campus. Your career services, alumni, or school may post fliers or send out emails about upcoming events. Attending an on-campus networking event gives you the advantage of being around other students and having something in common with outsiders in attendance.

An excellent way to begin meeting with professionals in your industry is to go off campus and meet them at industry events and meetings.

Getting Started:

1. Visit **Meetup.com**.

2. Search for a meetup either by your interest/industry or your area code.

3. RSVP for one of the meetups.

4. Go alone so you'll be more open to networking with others.

5. Bring your business cards **(SEE #43)**, prepare your 30-second pitch **(SEE #23)**, and dress the part **(SEE #46)**.

6. Meet as many people as you can.

7. For more networking tips, visit **101Grads.com/Networking-Tips**.

❏ 29. Master Microsoft Excel & PowerPoint

In the business world people don't communicate with 30-page term papers or multiple choice exams. They communicate using Microsoft Office. Even if you have an iPod, iPhone, and MacBook, we're sure you're familiar with Microsoft Office and the suite of tools it offers such as Word, Excel, and PowerPoint. Creating a Word document, using spell check, and expanding margins to make a 20-page paper look like 30 pages—these are only the tip of the Microsoft Office iceberg.

Microsoft Excel does more than just hold first names in column A, last names in column B, and email addresses in column C. It's way more powerful than that and can be used for a variety of tasks including business planning, personal budgeting, scenario planning, and contact management. Learning how to use Excel formulas (such as SUM, COUNTIF, or LOOKUP) is the next level and can accelerate number crunching and organizing information both in your personal and professional lives.

As you will find later with public speaking **(SEE #33)**, you will always have to present yourself and your ideas, and Microsoft PowerPoint is a powerful way to communicate them visually. When you step into a professional environment you will have to get comfortable making presentations to colleagues and clients. Mastering PowerPoint will let you develop some impressive tools and tips to set yourself apart.

Getting Started:

1. Look for a computer class on campus or at a local junior college to learn these technologies in more depth. Your campus may have tutorials at the computer lab as well.

2. If there isn't a class on campus, you can also find Microsoft tutorials online at **MIStupid.com/tutorials**.

3. You can also get officially certified in Microsoft Office. For more information, visit **101Grads.com/Microsoft-Certification**.

❏ 30. Make A List Of All Your Skills

Do you know all the skills you have? Being able to list your skills makes it easier for employers to decide whether or not to hire you. It helps you to prepare to speak articulately and persuasively about yourself.

Most job seekers find that talking about themselves makes them uncomfortable. Preparing your 30-second pitch **(SEE #23)** will help give you the confidence to introduce yourself. Now you want to extend this by taking an inventory of all your skills and strengths.

You'll want to use this inventory to craft your story (all your features and benefits) so interviewers will clearly understand how your qualifications will meet their needs. The better and more prepared your story, the more competitive a candidate you will be.

To develop your story, you'll use a marketable skills profile. A marketable skills profile is the output of the process that puts your skills and experiences together concisely. It also helps you develop a script to use in interviews and throughout your job search. Consider your profile as a list of assertions (headlines) about yourself.

Getting Started:

1. Make a list of your work, volunteer, and educational experience.

2. Write down at least 3 tasks/achievements performed during each of those experiences.

3. Write down 3 skills utilized while performing each task. (e.g. event planning: budgeting, organizing, leading)

4. Choose those skills that are relevant to the position you are seeking and highlight them in your résumé, cover letter, and interviews.

5. To learn more about how to create a marketable skills profile, visit **101Grads.com/Marketable-Skills-Profile**.

6. Also check out **SkillShare.com** for courses to develop new personal and professional skills.

Example: _public speaking_   5._____

1._____   6._____

2._____   7._____

3._____   8._____

4._____   9._____

❏ 31. Intern With 2 Companies

Internships are a great way to "date" an industry, company or job function before you decide to get further committed. They usually take place during the summer for a 3-month period and they can be paid or unpaid. The greatest value of an internship is work experience. It can be an opportunity to apply everything you're learning in school. Or it can give you an introduction to something you know nothing about. Either way, an internship is hugely valuable.

Besides exposure and experience, there are future financial benefits to doing internships. According to the National Association of Colleges and Employers, 42.3% of the seniors who had internship experience and applied for a job received at least one job offer. Conversely, only 30.7% of seniors without internship experience who applied for a job received an offer. And overall, students in the Class of 2010 who had internships received an average salary offer of $41,580. Meanwhile, their classmates who didn't take internships received an average starting salary offer of $34,601.

The number one thing a potential employer is going to look for upon graduation is work experience—not your GPA, school name, or major. An internship lets you develop work experience so that you don't get caught in the work experience trap—how do I gain work experience if everyone requires work experience to work? In order to get an summer internship, start looking for one in January and February. If you need to earn money during the summer, look into school-year internships or see about part-time summer internships.

Getting Started:

1. Work on your résumé and cover letter.

2. Visit your career center for feedback and guidance about how and where to apply.

3. Ask members of your Career Team **(SEE #57)** if they know of any opportunities that align with your career interests.

4. Also check out **InternQueen.com** and **SummerInternships.com** for opportunities in your career of interest.

5. If you don't like your first summer internship, try something different next summer.

❏ 32. Earn A Certificate Or License Relevant To Your Career Path

Each spring, hundreds of thousands of college graduates flood the job market. How will you distinguish yourself from the masses? One of the best ways is by earning an additional certificate or license in the field of your choice before graduation.

If you do what everyone else does, you can expect to get what everyone else gets. And right now, college graduates are getting the short end of the stick. Set yourself apart from the pack by acquiring career-related education during college rather than afterward. At the end of the day, that qualification may be more valuable to your career than your college diploma.

There are many certifications and licenses that would mean more to employers than your major and minor. Most of them don't have an age or college graduation requirement. If you're going into the financial sector you can explore becoming a Certified Public Accountant or Certified Financial Planner or if you're going into operations you can consider getting a Six Sigma certificate. Many entry-level employees don't earn certifications like these until a few years into their career, once they've committed to a certain line of work, but you can change the game by getting your certification or license now.

Getting Started:

1. Ask someone in your field of interest what kinds of certifications or licenses people in their line of work earn.

2. Visit the websites of companies you're interested in and read Executive Team bios to see what certificates and licenses they have.

3. Also visit **101Grads.com/Certifications** for a listing of certifications and licenses and then find a program or class near you.

4. Sign up for the appropriate training and exam and pass the certification or licensing test.

❐ 33. Give A Public Speech

Knowing how to present yourself and your ideas will always be a valuable skill, whether you are dating, interviewing, raising money for a start-up, or trying to sell to a new client at work. Successful public speaking allows you to connect with people who may view the world differently than you, gain their trust, invite them into your life, and show them the world as you see it.

At the same time, fear of public speaking is one of the most common responses in any survey of common anxieties. We want to be famous, but we don't want all eyes on us. We want to be heard, but we don't want to speak up. We want others to believe what we believe, but we're afraid to share why we believe it.

Public speaking is the space where the private world meets the public. Too often, people giving a public presentation simply hide behind their PowerPoint presentations and scripts. But you can learn how to share your story confidently and persuasively with those who are willing to listen.

Learning how to speak in public is one of the most powerful tools at your disposal. The ability to effectively communicate, persuade, dissuade, convince, debate, and articulate your ideas is essential in every aspect of life. Like powerful writing, speech has the power to influence one million people or just one person. And it affords you the opportunity to negotiate who you are in relation to other people and to the world as a whole. Use it to your greatest advantage!

Getting Started:

1. Write a speech or create a presentation about something you genuinely care about.

2. Record your speech and post it online, either on **YouTube.com** or **Facebook.com**.

3. Offer to host or present at an on-campus event or speak at a K-12 class about college to develop your public speaking skills.

4. Check out **ToastMasters.org** for classes on public speaking. Your campus may have a chapter.

❐ 34. Learn How To Use Photoshop Or iMovie

Have you ever doodled in class? What if you could turn those doodles into digital masterpieces? Almost every book cover, logo, billboard, and magazine you've seen has been designed in Adobe Photoshop. It's a powerful tool that allows you to visually express the ideas you have in your mind. Whether you want to create a header for your blog or website **(SEE #37)** or you want to touch up your **Facebook.com** profile picture, this is the best tool to use.

Apple's iMovie program makes it easy to create movies using footage captured on your web cam or a digital camera. Most people who post on Youtube.com simply post raw footage straight from their camera with no editing. With iMovie you can add transitions, music, text, and other effects to tell a compelling story. In your personal life it can be used to create a great Happy Birthday video for a distant friend or a Valentine's Day video for someone you love. Professionally, it will allow you capture a presentation or idea that can be spread widely without you having to physically present it over and over.

Since video and images are the primary ways our generation consumes information, it's important to know how to use these mediums to communicate. These two technologies will expand the ways you can communicate your ideas in personal and professional settings.

Getting Started:

1. Search your course listings for classes that teach you how to use multi-media technologies like Photoshop or iMovie. If your campus doesn't offer classes, then search for off-campus courses that you can take as an alternative Spring Break **(SEE #98)**.

2. Design a logo for your website **(SEE #37)** or a flyer for your event **(SEE #85)**.

3. Create a video to help you with one of the other *101 Things* such as raise $1,000 for a cause you believe in **(SEE #84)** or do a public speech **(SEE #33)**.

4. Add them to your portfolio on your website **(SEE #39)**.

❐ 35. Learn HTML & CSS

We are in the internet age and in order to have a voice in this world, you have to speak the languages—HTML, CSS, PHP, AJAX, .NET, and Javascript. You can start with the basics: HTML and CSS. These are the backbone of every web page you visit from **Facebook.com** to **Google.com** to your very own blog.

HTML stands for Hyper Text Markup Language. Markups are to web pages as punctuation is to an essay. They allow web browsers like Internet Explorer, Firefox, Safari, and Chrome to read the HTML and display it properly as a page. Some common text markups that you use in word processing, including bold, italics, underlines, tables and hyperlinks are used in HTML as the fundamental building blocks of all websites.

CSS stands for Cascading Style Sheets. It defines the appearance and layout of text and other objects in the HTML such as embedded YouTube videos, menus, bulleted lists, and tables. In the same way that you can edit font, font size, font spacing, and margins on your essays, CSS allows you to do that online.

HTML and CSS work together to create a common language by which the web communicates and displays information. Like any language used by human beings, these languages allow content creators to curate their content and express themselves in unique ways.

Getting Started:

1. Search your course listings for classes that teach you how to use HTML, CSS, PHP, JavaScript, and/or AJAX.

2. Test these languages out as you develop your blog or website **(SEE #37)**.

3. Visit **101Grads.com/Learn-HTML** for basic HTML tutorials.

❐ 36. Take The Gallup *StrengthsFinder 2.0*

We live in a world that teaches us to focus on our weaknesses instead of our strengths. If you end a semester with 5 As and 1 F, what would your teachers and parents tell you to focus on? They would likely encourage you to spend time and energy bringing up your F so that you can be well-rounded in a variety of subjects. That's the formula to becoming a jack of all trades, master of none. Now imagine a teacher or parent who pushed you further and further in a subject that you've demonstrated greatness in. You may face challenges at first, but you will only get stronger and stronger over time.

The Gallup *StrengthsFinder 2.0* is a tool that will help you identify your top 5 strengths and give you ways to integrate them in every aspect of your life. Some of the strengths include focus, woo, achiever, maximizer, ideation, and relator. Inside the book, you will find a code to take an online test that will generate your own strengths assessment. The goal is to help you build your life around your strengths, rather than focus on what you're not good at. It's impossible to be strong at everything so we should find what we're strong at and get so strong that our weaknesses pale in comparison.

Getting Started:

1. Learn more about the Gallup *StrengthsFinder 2.0* at
    101Grads.com/Strengths-Finder.

2. Buy the book at **101Grads.com/Strengths-Finder-Book**.

3. Look through the 34 themes and guess what your
    strengths are.

4. Take the online test and get your results.

5. Read the chapters in the book related to your top 5
    strengths.

6. Eliminate or change daily activities and roles that don't
    speak to your strengths.

❐ 37. Start A Blog Or Website

One of the best ways to position yourself in the world is by publishing high-quality content on a particular subject that you are passionate about. Today, you no longer need to work through the publishing establishment in order to do this. You can connect with an audience directly by creating a personal website and by blogging. People create websites for different purposes—personal, professional, fame, or financial. You don't need to be Mark Zuckerberg to create your own website, but you do need to build your brand online.

You probably know already that blogs cover a wide range of subjects. In your blog, you could document your daily life, share your passion for a niche subject, or teach others how to do something you know well. If you choose to write frequently you can start to develop a following, but the primary purpose of the blog or website is to brand yourself as a valuable person. When you have an insight about life or business, an accomplishment that reflects your abilities, or just something fun to share, your blog is a perfect space to do so.

In addition to writing about subjects you are passionate about, your blog or website can give visitors access to a portfolio of your best work, your bio, and your résumé. In this way, they'll get to know you as well and as fully as you want them to. Later on in this chapter, we mention a number of other ways to develop your online brand such as buying your own domain name **(SEE #38)** and cleaning up your **Facebook.com** profile **(SEE #40)**.

Getting Started:

1. Determine what the content and purpose of your blog or website will be.

2. Create a blog or website for free using **Wordpress.com**, **Blogger.com**, **Weebly.com**, or **Tumblr.com**.

3. Create or post 4 pieces of content that reflect who you are (e.g. a blog post, photos, your résumé as a PDF, and a YouTube video that inspires you).

4. Email a few of your close friends the link to your site and ask them for feedback.

❑ 38. Buy Your Own Domain Name

Google yourself and see what comes up. Almost every employer, potential life partner, and person you meet will search for you on Google before they decide to deepen their relationship with you. It is important that you know and control what they find. You want to shape people's first impression of you online just as much as you do in person with your speech, appearance, and demeanor.

In most cases, your **Facebook.com** profile will be one of the first things that comes up **(SEE #40)**. We recommend that you delete or untag yourself from any incriminating photos. But you can only customize **Facebook.com** so much. Having your own domain name allows you to control where someone goes when they enter your name into Google. You can forward them to material that you control such as your personal website, your blog, your bio, or your portfolio. Though you can't control everything out there about you on the web, you should own www.yourname.com.

Getting Started:

1. Go to **GoDaddy.com** and buy your domain name for about $11 per year.

2. If your name is already taken use your middle initial or buy a .net or .org.

3. If you don't have a website or blog yet, link your domain to something about you online that presents your personal brand in a positive manner. It can be an article written about you by someone else or a link to your profile on a reputable social network site such as **LinkedIn.com**.

❐ 39. Create A Portfolio

During your undergraduate experience you will create approximately 20-30 projects, papers, or presentations. Your portfolio is simply a presentation of your best five best pieces of work—some of which you will create as you complete the *101 Things*. Your portfolio can include a variety of work samples such as:

- Projects or papers you are very proud of and got a great grade on;

- Marketing plan and/or flyers you created for an event you produced **(SEE #85)**;

- Business plan you wrote for a business plan competition **(SEE #66)**;

- Article you wrote and published for the campus newspaper **(SEE #12)**;

- Letters of recommendations from professors and other professionals **(SEE #53)**.

As you begin exploring various career paths and going on interviews you will find that people want to see what you've actually produced. Tangible quantitative and qualitative results speak to your ability to get things done and this is what employers are seeking in an employee. Therefore, the most valuable thing you can bring into your interview is your portfolio; rather than talking about the quality of your work, you can actually show it to them. This single action will set you apart from other candidates who only bring copies of their one-page résumé.

Getting Started:

1. Sort and think through all of the amazing projects you've done so far that you are proud of and gave your best effort on.

2. Identify 5 or more items that show the breadth and depth of your work—make sure to include various types of work samples (e.g. essay, PowerPoint presentation, business plan, etc.).

3. Scan and print 3 copies of each in color on high-quality paper.

4. Compile them into packets or a professional leather folder.

5. Upload the ones that you can to your blog or website for potential employers to see.

❒ 40. Clean Up Your Facebook.com Profile

You've probably heard this 1,000 times already, but **ALL EMPLOYERS CHECK FACEBOOK.COM.**

We know that you just want a fun place online where you can post crazy pictures from parties and other fun campus nights, but do you want those photos to be the deciding factor in whether or not you get hired?

Everything you do online can be traced back to you. That goes for all websites, not just **Facebook.com**.

Facebook doesn't make this easy, but there are two ways to effectively clean up your profile.

Getting Started:

1. You can change your privacy settings and sort out your **Facebook.com** friends. For information on changing your Facebook privacy settings, visit **101Grads.com/Facebook-Privacy**.

2. Untag yourself from any photos or notes that you think would appear as inappropriate in the eyes of a potential employer.

3. Start using your **Facebook.com** status updates to brand yourself by posting quality content, comments, and links about things related to your career path.

4. If having a free-flowing **Facebook.com** account is extremely important to you, create an account under an alias so that people can't find you by your given name.

☐ 41. Create A LinkedIn.com Account

Facebook.com is for fun.

LinkedIn.com is for professionals.

LinkedIn.com can serve many purposes for you. It allows you to build a professional webpage, with your profile appearing alongside those of professors, CEOs and other leaders in their field. It lets you search for and find people who work at your target companies or organizations. It lets you ask for and get recommendations from people you've worked with in the past to validate your experience. **LinkedIn.com** offers you the opportunity to create a résumé-like profile online that is safe for employers, colleagues, and mentors to view.

When you Google yourself **(SEE #42)** and don't find much, **LinkedIn.com** provides a great way to start building your brand and network online. **LinkedIn.com** profiles rank high on **Google.com** searches. Also, there are over 75 million **LinkedIn.com** members, so you'll find most of your network online.

Getting Started:

1. Go to **LinkedIn.com** and sign up for a new account.

2. Complete your profile and make sure your profile progress bar is at 100%.

3. Connect with your network by using the email search feature.

4. Join **LinkedIn.com** groups related to your industry to find out more information and network with professionals. You can find the most useful groups by seeing the memberships of others.

5. Answer and ask questions on **LinkedIn.com** Answers.

6. Continue to maximize your profile by visiting **101Grads.com/LinkedIn**.

☐ 42. Google Yourself & Edit Your Online Image

Just like you Google a company you are researching, employers will Google you to find out more about you, beyond your résumé.

Do you have embarrassing photos you forgot were online? Tweets you would like to forget?

Everything you do online can be traced back to you. That goes for *all* websites.

You want employers to easily find you online, but in a positive light. Take control of the items people will find when they Google you, especially those that appear on your first page of search results.

Getting Started:

1. Go to **Google.com** and type in your name. If you have a more common name, you may want to add a little more detail like your hometown or college.

2. Click on every link that's related to you on the first 10 pages of Google.

3. If you find any information that does not put you in a good light, try to delete it.

4. If it's a social media site, try logging on and deleting the information.

5. If it's a website that is owned by someone else, try contacting them, requesting that the information be removed.

6. Repeat this process for Google Image Search, Video Search, Blog Search, News Search, etc.

7. Also visit **BeyondCredentials.com** to post a professional profile if **LInkedIn.com** isn't sufficient.

❒ 43. Get Business Cards

Whether you're in a social setting, a professional setting, or just at the grocery store, business cards are essential to initiating a long-term relationship.

If you want to appear like a professional, especially when networking, you need business cards. You don't have to have a job, own a business, or even major in business to have a business card. If you're looking for a job, you need a business card.

Business cards should communicate who you are, what you do, how to contact you, and where to go to learn more about you.

What do you put on your business card if you're just a student? Glad you asked. We've included a sample card for you to model yours after the next page.

Getting Started:

1. Go to **VistaPrint.com** or **Moo.com**.

2. Design your business card using our model below.

3. Start by ordering 250 cards. It only costs $10 and they'll last quite awhile.

Sarah Sociology
Enthusiastlc, Highly Organized, Hard Working
and Dependable College Senior
Looking for an Internship
in the Field of Event Planning

IVY University, P.O. Box 1234   (123) 456-7890
New York, NY 10000   Sarah2@IVYU.edu

❒ 44. Get A Personalized Email Address

Get an email address that is professional and easy to remember so employers can email you. If you have a clever, cute or provocative email address like cutiepie@domain.com, yankeesfan@domain.com, or sexkitten@domain.com, get a new email address!

Your email address may be clever, memorable, and fun, but it can also cause your prospective employer to think, "I can't believe someone would actually list this email address on her résumé, let alone use it to correspond with me. Will she use the same poor judgment on the job if I hire her?"

Getting Started:

1. Use your school's or your alumni association's domain name (e.g. student@alumni.college.edu), if possible.

2. Create a separate email for your job search with one of the free email providers like Google or Yahoo. For more information about free email systems check out **101Grads.com/Free-Email-Systems**.

3. Use your name or initials in your email address. That may be a challenge when using a free email system, but jsmith1234@domain.com is much better than marathonlover1@domain.com.

❑ 45. Record A New Voicemail Message

Wondering why you are not hearing back from employers? Maybe it's not your résumé, it's your voicemail message.

Make sure your voicemail message on your main telephone line is appropriate for receiving calls from employers. You cannot afford to use an audio clip from Sponge Bob Square Pants on your voicemail. Sure, you may think it's funny, but employers won't.

Your message should be clean and simple. Here is a sample voicemail message you can use:

> *"Hi, this is (your name).*
> *I can't answer the phone*
> *so please leave your name,*
> *number and a brief message.*
> *I will get back to you soon.*
> *Thanks for calling."*

Getting Started:

1. Delete your voicemail message if it contains music, has a lot of background noise, or cannot be clearly understood.

2. Use the voicemail template above to record a new message.

3. Keep the message short.

4. Return all calls from potential employers as soon as possible.

❏ 46. Find 2 Quality Business Suits

On campus, your wardrobe can consist of jeans, t-shirts, hoodies, and flip-flops or sneakers. Or maybe that's only if you felt like dressing up: otherwise you go to class in your pajamas.

Well, all of that needs to change.

To be seen as professional, you have to look the part. You have to dress professionally not just for interviews but also for networking events, company presentations, and sometimes class.

For gentlemen, a business outfit consists of a dress shirt, a tie, dress pants, sport coat, and dress shoes. Ladies should have a skirt or pants, suit, blouse, dress shoes and a simple handbag. Jewelry should be either absent or very restrained. As you go along, you will want to find some business casual outfits in addition to two quality business suits.

Getting Started:

1. Get two quality suits with the necessary accessories. These are available at a full range of price points from Target and Wal-Mart on up.

2. If you can't afford a suit, women can check out **DressForSuccess.org** and men can visit **CareerGear.org.**

3. Get your suits tailored to fit you properly. A good fit goes a long way to upgrading a less expensive outfit.

4. Wear dress shoes. Ladies, business heels are nice, otherwise wear simple flats. If you wear heels, make sure they aren't flashy.

5. Be sure to have your hair cut, your breath fresh, finger nails clean, and most importantly, a smile on your face.

6. For more on what to wear, visit **101Grads.com/Dress-To-Impress.**

❐ 47. Create & Edit Your Résumé

No matter what you may hear, the "old-fashioned" résumé isn't dead yet. It's true that there are many online social networks that allow you to create professional profiles that employers use to search for potential candidates. However, at the core of these sites is information that is also found on a résumé, such as work experience, education, skills, and contact information.

If an employer finds you through these sites, they will ask you to send them a copy of your résumé. Your résumé still plays a key role in getting a job interview. Not only does a résumé let an employer learn more about you, it also allows you to organize your experiences and begin to create personal talking points for job interviews.

Two of the biggest mistakes people make with résumés are not customizing and not editing. Each résumé you write should be tailored to the job you are seeking. This can be done by creating a core résumé and then customizing it with relevant work experience, activities, classes, and skills.

Your résumé MUST be 100% error free, otherwise it will be 100% rejected.

Getting Started:

1. Find a résumé template online. Look for entry level or recent graduate templates.

2. Fill out basic contact, education, employment, activities, and skills information.

3. Write three bullet point sentences under each job and activity you listed stating an accomplishment, not just a duty.

4. Bring your résumé to your career services office for review.

5. Have a mentor and/or a professional in the industry review your résumé.

6. For more on résumé writing, visit **101Grads.com/Resume**.

❐ 48. Post Your Résumé On 3 Job Boards

Every day, thousands of jobs are posted online. Searching online for a job has become as easy as checking your email, but don't get lulled into the false sense of security that the Internet offers. You can't passively wait for the Internet to provide you a job. It is important for you to take your job search as seriously as you would the job you're seeking.

Keep in mind that there are thousands of other people visiting **Monster.com**, **CareerBuilder.com**, and **Indeed.com** to find a job. Therefore, you are not just competing against other college students, but all job seekers. An online job search will become a waste of time if not done effectively.

By posting on job boards you are letting the market know that you are valuable and available even if you aren't actively seeking. If your résumé is a perfect fit, you might get called by a potential employer and they may hold your résumé for when the time is right for both of you.

Getting Started:

1. Choose 3 jobs boards, including one general job posting site and two sites specific to your industry.

2. Do keyword, industry, and job title searches. If you are an aerospace engineer and you like to write, you might search for "aerospace, engineer, writer, writing, technical, proposal" rather than just "aerospace engineer."

3. Make sure you read the entire job posting, and comply with all the requests listed.

4. Save a copy of every job posting, along with your cover letter and the résumé you sent, organized by the month.

5. For a list of general and industry-specific job sites, visit **101Grads.com/Job-Search-Websites**.

☐ 49. Conduct 3 Informational Interviews

If you want an advantage over other job seekers, you have to conduct informational interviews. Informational interviews involve meeting with professionals who are doing what you want to do and asking them what it takes to be successful in their field.

Some of the benefits are:

1. **Networking**: As soon as you interview them, you become part of their network. People enjoy feeling valued and there's no better way to show that than by interviewing them.

2. **Insider information**: A well-conducted interview will give you honest first-person answers about what it's like to work in your industry, something that other forms of research cannot provide.

3. **Access to the hidden job market**: You are "promoted" to the top of their list next time they hear of a job opening because you've shown them initiative and passion.

Getting Started:

1. Use **LinkedIn.com** or your alumni office to identify people who are working in the field you want to work in.

2. Send at least three people an email expressing your interest in speaking with them for 10-15 minutes to learn more about their career and company. Attach your résumé.

3. Research each person as thoroughly as possible so that you are informed when you contact them and can ask great questions when you meet them. Google them, check out their personal and company websites, get familiar with any writing they've done and any recognition they've received in terms of awards or news stories.

4. Approach the meeting like an interview without the pressure.

5. Let them know your college and career timeline.

6. Follow up with a thank-you note or card **(SEE #81)**.

❒ 50. Do A Mock Interview

Mock interviews often get a bad rep from job seekers, but it's usually from the people who don't get hired.

They are the best way to get comfortable before an interview and this is especially true when you have a professional critiquing you. Would you rather have a helpful career professional pointing out your mistakes or a recruiter during your actual interview?

Most people think, "What's so hard about an interview? All you have to do is answer questions about yourself. You can wing it." No. A job interview is about creating a great first impression coupled with proving to a potential employer that you are a good fit for them. They want to know that you know as much about them as they are seeking to learn about you. It's not as easy as it sounds.

The goal of a mock interview isn't to have you sound rehearsed, but to polish your presentation.

Getting Started:

1. Go to your career services department on campus or hire a career coach.

2. Bring your résumé and cover letter with you, so that the interviewer can ask relevant questions.

3. Wear what you would wear to an interview so that you'll have feedback on whether what you are wearing is appropriate.

4. Prepare for the mock interview as if you were going on an actual interview.

5. Videotape your interview.

6. Watch the video to review what you did right and wrong.

☐ 51. Know Your Answers To The Top 20 Interview Questions

What are your greatest strengths? What are your greatest weaknesses? What relevant experience do you have? If I asked one of your team members or co-workers about you, what would they say? What motivates you to do a good job? How much are you looking to earn? Tell me a suggestion you have made that was implemented. What is your greatest achievement to date? Why should I hire you?

These are just a few of the top 20 interview questions that you should be prepared to answer with confidence. They aren't as straightforward as a multiple choice test. There is no right answer—there is only your best answer. Being able to respond to these questions with confidence in the moment takes self-exploration and practice. Confidence combined with solid information will be more persuasive than your résumé, GPA, or college name alone.

The biggest mistake any job seeker can make is to apply for whatever is available without first asking themselves the questions above. Your unique answers to these questions can help you determine which companies to apply to, rather than applying to any company and then hoping your answers align with who they are looking for. For instance, if you want to earn $50,000 out of college and a particular job is only offering $30,000, you can save everyone time by not applying. Focus on the companies and positions that match who you are and what you're looking for.

Getting Started:

1. Visit **101Grads.com/Interview-Questions** to see the top 20 interview questions and answer them in a Microsoft Word document.

2. Rehearse your answers in the bathroom mirror or on a web cam.

3. Use your answers in mock interviews **(SEE #50)**.

4. Keep practicing until your answers resonate as true to you.

❏ 52. Prepare 5 Unique Questions For Every Interview

Here's something you probably didn't realize—job interviews are like dates.

If you treat your interview like it's a date, you'll realize the key is chemistry. Chemistry during an interview comes from having a good conversation with your interviewer.

Too often, during an interview the person doing most of the talking is you and not the employer.

That needs to change. You need to ask questions to show employers your interest in the company and to see if they are a good fit for you too.

The last job interview question you may be asked is: "What can I answer for you?"

Prepare at least five specific questions of your own to ask ahead of time. Your questions should show the recruiter that you have in-depth knowledge of the company, its competitors, and the industry at large.

Getting Started:

1. Perform in-depth company research to ask questions that show you've done your homework **(SEE #55)**.

2. Prepare at least 5 questions and keep them on a pad of paper that you bring to the interview. For a list of strong questions to ask during an interview, visit **101Grads.com/ Interview-Questions-To-Ask**.

3. You don't have to wait until the interviewer asks you for questions if an opportunity arises earlier in the interview.

❑ 53. Get 3 References Or Recommendations

When it comes to products and services, word of mouth is the best form of marketing there is. When you hear about a movie, band, new technology, or restaurant from a friend, you are more likely to consider trying it. You can use this psychological tool to your advantage when it comes to your career as well.

Throughout college you work with many people, including classmates, student leaders, professors, alumni, and community leaders. All of these interactions will offer you the opportunity to make a lasting impression, but you must take advantage of that opportunity. If you just show up with the intention of getting by, that won't be the case. If you come with the intention of doing your best, you will stand out.

When you do stand out, the best way to benefit from your efforts is through a reference or letter of recommendation. You will definitely need these if you apply to graduate school or for a scholarship, but they are also valuable when applying for jobs. Hearing about your performance from a professor or an employer speaks volumes; it says that a professional is willing to vouch for you and your potential.

Getting Started:

1. Identify professionals who have been impressed by the quality of your work and contributions.

2. Call or meet in person to request a reference or letters of recommendation from those people. Make sure that their title is included and if possible, ask them to write the letter on their official letterhead.

3. Add the documents to your portfolio.

4. If the person you would like to approach is on **LinkedIn.com**, send them a reference request through the **LinkedIn.com** website. Their recommendation will then appear on your **LinkedIn.com** page to enhance your online professional brand.

❐ 54. Meet With A Career Advisor Each Semester

The best place to begin exploring your career options is your career services department. Remember that place they showed you in freshman orientation? Well, it's probably still there. (You may want to check the campus map, just to be sure.)

Career centers have earned poor reputations, mostly unfairly. That's because graduates who do not get a job while still in college hold them responsible for their failures. But you're going to prove that reputation wrong. So it's time to find out how to make the most of your college's career services department.

Career centers have tons of professional development programs and resources such as mock interview opportunities, job search engines, résumé writing and interviewing workshops, career fairs, personality assessment tools, and more. The only way to even begin to tap into all of these resources is by visiting your career center.

Getting Started:

1. Visit your career center and ask about all of the resources it provides. For a list of resources your career services department probably provides, visit **101Grads.com/ Career-Services**.

2. Set up an appointment with a counselor to explore your career goals and review your résumé and cover letter.

3. Sign up for access to their online job boards and email lists about career fairs, seminars, and other programs.

❒ 55. Do Company Research

A potential employer's needs may be communicated to you by a recruiter or listed in the job description. But other needs—the "hidden agenda"—are left unstated. Uncovering the employer's unstated needs through diligent research can give you a tangible competitive advantage.

Don't take shortcuts. A thorough understanding of a company's product lines, organization, history, successes, failures, goals, problems, and initiatives will enable you to ask intelligent questions during the interview, and tailor your responses to the interviewer's needs.

Few candidates take the time to figure out what a company's unstated needs are. Doing so can make a huge difference between you and other candidates, even those who are more experienced. Take the time to do diligent research —it will be time well spent.

Getting Started:

1. Visit the company's website and read through every page in it.

2. Read the company's annual report and press releases.

3. Research the company online at **Vault.com**, **Hoovers.com**, and **WetFeet.com**.

4. Visit your school's library where you can access more company databases and publications for free as a student.

5. Ask a librarian to help you with your research. They will show you how to research effectively and efficiently.

6. For a more comprehensive list of things you should know about the organization, industry, position, and the interviewer before an interview, visit **101Grads.com/ Interview-Research**.

❐ 56. Attend At Least 2 Career Fairs

The assumption that everyone makes is that you'll get a job that somehow relates to your college major. But remember that things don't always work out so neatly.

There are many job opportunities that are available to all majors. Explore these opportunities by visiting at least two career fairs. There are many opportunities to attend career fairs both on and off campus. The key is to be proactive and look for them on your own.

Keep in mind that each department at your school may have their own career fair, but they are open to all majors. Also, local cities and towns have career fairs. Industries, companies, and the government also have public career fairs that you can attend.

Getting Started:

1. Search around campus for postings about career fairs or ask your career advisor **(SEE #54)** and the career services center.

2. Look online and in local newspapers for upcoming career fairs.

3. Prepare for the career fair by getting a list of companies attending and researching them.

4. Customize your résumé for at least 3 employers that will be at the career fair.

5. Take extra résumés with you for additional companies you'll speak with.

6. For advice on how to make the most of a career fair, visit **101Grads.com/Career-Fairs**.

❐ 57. Recruit A Career Team

Do you feel like you're all alone in your job search? Build a team to help you! We're not talking about hiring people to write your résumé, or getting a career coach, or finding a double to go on interviews for you.

What we mean is that you have to let others know that you are looking for a job. If you tell everyone you know or have ever met that you are looking for a job, there are bound to be people who can help you make connections faster than you can alone. If you met with your career advisor **(SEE #54)**, you already have one person on your team, but keep in mind that advisors serve hundreds of students. Now is the time to expand your team to other people who know you well and are willing to help. Whereas your personal board of directors **(SEE #24)** is more holistic, your career team is primarily focused on helping with your job search, though it may include members of your personal board of directors.

Gathering teammates isn't as challenging as you think. It just takes a bit of courage and time. Your team should include an upperclassman going into the same field, a recent alum, an older alum, someone at the career center, a professor, and perhaps a family friend or relative. Don't wait until the last semester of senior year to build your team, as it will be too late. Start building your team today!

Getting Started:

1. Make a list of friends, relatives, neighbors, professors, former classmates, employers, co-workers, and others who you think may know something about your desired career path.

2. Reach out to everyone on your list and ask them to help you. You can do this through phone calls, emails, and by meeting them in person.

3. For an email template to help you recruit, visit **101Grads.com/Career-Team.**

4. When you reach out to your team, let them know as much as you can about yourself and what kind of job and industry interests you.

5. Follow up each response with a handwritten thank-you note **(SEE #81)** and an update on your job search progress.

❏ 58. Read A New Industry-Related Article Every Day For 30 Days

The suggestion to read anything outside of class assignments may make you cringe, but this will help you get a job.

Employers are always looking for employees that are well rounded and know what's going on in the industry. You don't have to be able to name all the CEOs of the top 50 companies in your industry, but you do have to know enough about the major headlines of the day.

Reading an industry publication keeps you informed and able to hold up your end of the conversation during networking events and job interviews.

Getting Started:

1. Find 3 industry-related publications by asking professors, professionals, and librarians.

2. Sign up for subscriptions. Many publications offer student discounts or you can access them through the library for free.

3. Bookmark the publications' websites or pick one as your homepage so you can easily get updates when you go online. Another option is to "like" the publications' Facebook fan page to get automatic updates in your personal Facebook feed.

4. Subscribe to the publication's RSS feed so you can stay informed on the latest news.

5. Create Google Alerts for your target industry, company, and publications at **Google.com/Alerts**. This will create a filter that pulls articles based on specific keywords related to your target industry or companies.

HOW WILL YOU INVEST 216,000 MINUTES?

Money

"College is the best route to wealth." This has long been the accepted wisdom, but it never really was true. If that were true, you would expect the wealthiest people in the world to all be college graduates. Well, they're not. In fact, only 2 out of the 10 wealthiest people in the world graduated from college. College may once have been the best route to financial security, if not wealth, but as tuition continues to rise while employment rates and salaries for recent graduates decline, the investment isn't as lucrative as it used to be.

Now, our message isn't "Drop out of college and you'll get rich." The average college graduate makes a million more dollars over the course of their lifetime than someone who just graduates only from high school. The lesson is that the world's wealthiest people are focused on creating value and creating jobs, whereas education often teaches us to focus on capturing value or just getting a job.

One of the big reasons people go to college is to increase their chances of making money. However, if that is your primary goal, a more direct route may be to just learn how money works so that you can create it, and manage it. Though we're in school for what seems like forever, most of us are financially illiterate. We don't know how money works: we don't know how to create it and we don't know how to manage it. Given that, we get caught up in the rat race trying to make as much money as we possibly can in hopes that our incomes will keep up with our expenses.

Let's start off by assessing your first major investment—college. A student at Harvard pays about $36,000 in tuition and $24,000 per year to cover the cost of living. If you multiply that by 4 years, you get $240,000—this will be well over a quarter million dollars when you add interest on any loans. Now let's say they are on campus 9 months out of the year, 20 days per month, for 5 hours each day. Over the course of 4 years, that's a total of 3,600 hours or 216,000 minutes. If you divide that the $240,000 by 216,000 minutes, a Harvard undergraduate is essentially paying $1.11 every minute they are on campus. Now do the calculation for your school.

As with any investment—a stock, bond, mutual fund, 401K— you want a return on your investment. Unfortunately, instead of earning a *return on their investment*, most college students are *returning home* after graduation to live with their parents again.

To ensure that you get a good return on the investment you've made in higher education, you have to ask yourself, "Am I maximizing each minute I spend on campus in a way that will yield more than $1.11 of value for me in the near future?" When you look at college as an investment, it changes the way you spend your time. Instead of wasting time playing Halo for 8 hours or sleeping in classes you don't care about, you will seek to invest in doing things that increase the value of your experience.

Your diploma is only valuable to the extent that you make it so, and that depends on what you do with your four years. Don't end up with an expensive piece of paper that says major debt and minor capital. The value of your piece of paper will be determined by your dash. What do we mean by "dash?" That's the line that comes between your birth date and your death date on your tombstone. It represents your life, what you created, experienced, and achieved.

College has a dash too—the dash between orientation and graduation. As certain as death is, the mere fact that you're reading this book makes us pretty certain that you're going to make it to the end of the college dash. But what will you have to show for this four year dash? If time is the most valuable asset you have, then your return on life will be determined by how you invest your time. In the same way, the value of your college degree will be determined by how you spend these four years of time.

If you maximize the dash, it will determine where the commas in your income fall. And the richness that college can add to your life includes the opportunities it offers to explore the road less traveled. When you examine the lives of the world's wealthiest people, none of them took conventional paths—dropouts and graduates included. Imagine if Bill Gates or Mark Zuckerberg had gone into investment banking or consulting like the rest of their peers. There would be no Microsoft and no **Facebook.com**. Use college as a safe space to create and fail, create and fail, create and fail, so that you can become not just a consumer in today's economy but also a creator of real value for others. Even if you don't want to be an entrepreneur, the person with the entrepreneurial mindset will always create more wealth in the long-run than someone with an employee-only mindset.

MILLIONAIRES CREATE LOTS OF

VALUE

FOR OTHERS AND THEN

KEEP

A FRACTION

❐ 59. Create A Budget

Got money? You need a budget.

Don't have any money? You still need a budget.

Budgets seem like such a drag, but an even bigger drag is not knowing what you're doing with your money and not having enough to enjoy the finer things in life. A budget allows you to keep tabs on your money and spend it on the things that matter to you.

A budget allows you to tell your money where to go instead of wondering where it went.

It is especially helpful when you want to pay down loans and avoid late fees and overdraft fees from credit cards and banks.

Getting Started:

1. Get a notebook, download the Microsoft Excel budget spreadsheet at **101Grads.com/Budget**, or setup an online budget at **Mint.com**.

2. At the top of the page, write down how much you have.

3. Write down everything you spend money on in a week including food, gas, coffee, gum, pizza, etc. If you earn any money, write that down as well. Also, don't forget to write down if you pay any bills during that time.

4. At the end of week, do a little bit of adding and subtracting to figure out how much you spent.

5. Make adjustments to your spending habits if you don't have any money left or are spending too much on one category.

❒ 60. Set Up Checking & Savings Accounts

Getting a handle on your finances doesn't require getting a stockbroker or a personal financial advisor—it's much simpler than that.

The first step is to set up your bank accounts to manage your money. Having a checking or savings account is the foundation upon which you establish your financial life. A checking account allows you to securely hold and easily withdraw money from your bank through checks and ATMs. A savings account enables you to save money and earn interest.

Managing your money while in college will help you make better decisions about spending versus saving money and it will set your finances on the right track.

Getting Started:

1. Determine what account features are important for your needs. For some ideas visit **101Grads.com/Banking-Needs**.

2. Meet with bank managers and ask questions to decide which bank and type of account is right for you. For questions to ask a bank, visit **101Grads.com/ Interviewing-Banks**.

3. Balance your checkbook every month.

4. Learn banking basics, such as writing a check, by visiting **101Grads.com/Banking-Basics**.

5. Keep tabs on your bank accounts by signing up for bank text and email alerts. You can get emails every day with your current balance and you have the bank alert you when your balance drops below a certain minimum.

❏ 61. Get Your Credit Reports & Scores

You may know how well you are doing academically, but do you know how you are doing financially?

Your credit reports and credit scores are like the report card and GPA for your financial life. A credit report shows whether you've been on time in paying your debts, such as credit card bills and auto loans. A credit score is the value that a rating agency attaches to your repayment history and debt levels: creditors use this credit score to judge if you are worthy of receiving credit.

If you have poor credit reports and low credit scores, you will be charged higher interest rates or may be rejected when you apply for loans or credit cards.

Many people think that there is just one credit report and one credit score, but there are 3, one from each of the credit bureaus (TransUnion, Equifax, and Experian). You must work with all three bureaus to improve your credit.

Getting Started:

1. Get all three credit reports for FREE at
   AnnualCreditReport.com.

2. You can also get all three credit scores from **MyFICO.com**.
   This may cost you some money, but it's well worth the
   investment.

3. Review your credit reports and fix any errors. If you find an
   error contact the credit bureau as soon as possible. Keep
   notes of everything they tell you and get confirmation
   numbers for the calls you make.

4. Do this every year to maintain good credit.

❒ 62. Eliminate Your Credit Card Debt

Be cautious of those credit cards they promote on campus in exchange for a free t-shirt. Nothing is free. The average college student graduates with $3,173 in credit card debt. Bad credit can hurt your ability to get a job, an apartment, and a loan for a home, car, or wedding.

You should never spend money that you haven't earned, therefore you should cut up all of your credit cards and build your credit by paying your cell phone bill and rent on time with money from your checking or savings account **(SEE #60)**.

You have the ability to create a strong debt-free financial foundation for your life as a college student if you properly manage your expenses and wait patiently to buy what you desire until you have the income to afford it. The last thing you need when you graduate is additional debt weighing you down as you are looking for your first job.

Getting Started:

1. Stop using your credit cards. Don't allow yourself to get into any more debt.

2. Talk to your creditors. Let them know that you acknowledge your debt and you will work in good faith to pay it off.

3. Write down all of the money you owe, when it's due, the minimum payment amount, and the interest rate. Use our payment tool to organize your debt at **101Grads.com/ Debt-Tool.**

4. Pay at least all of your minimum payments each month.

5. Use additional monies to start paying down your debts. Start with the debt with the smallest total.

6. Once the debt with the smallest total is paid off, continue with the next smallest debt.

7. Free up more money for credit card payments by revisiting your monthly budget. Set spending reduction goals for one or two cost categories.

8. Look to see if there are things you can do to increase your financial resources such as getting a part-time job, doing freelance work, or applying for additional scholarships **(SEE #13).**

❐ 63. Start A $1,000 Emergency Fund

In life, you have to expect the unexpected. When it comes to money, unexpected expenses can hit at any time. Whether it's your car breaking down, financial aid coming up short, losing your on-campus job, or having to fly home unexpectedly, there are times when you are going to need extra money. The best way to prepare for these unexpected expenses is to have an emergency fund you can draw on.

Start budgeting **(SEE #59)** and putting aside any extra money into an emergency fund with the goal of saving $1,000. This can go a long way to covering any unexpected expenses. Relying on credit cards or a loan will simply compound the problem. Instead, give yourself the security and peace of mind that comes from having an emergency fund.

Getting Started:

1. Create a S.M.A.R.T. goal **(SEE #87)** for saving $1,000.

2. Begin by saving $10 a week. If you can afford more, then save more.

3. Have your bank make an automatic transfer each week from your checking account into a savings account. This way you won't even notice it.

4. Turn your savings into a Certificate of Deposit (CD). This will pay a higher interest rate than a savings account but will still let you access the money when you truly need it.

❒ 64. Do Your Own Taxes

If you earn enough money, you're going to have to pay taxes or else you'll be running from the IRS. Since taxes can take up to 30% of your income, it is important to know how they are calculated and how you can save as much money as possible.

Doing your taxes feels like one more final exam. But there's one big difference: this grade is measured in cash. With a little research and time, you can ace this test and maybe even earn a nice check while doing it, in the form of a tax refund. Taxes aren't as challenging as they may seem, it just takes time to fill them out.

As a college student, you will probably be filling out the 1040EZ form. This is a simplified form that only applies to single or married people with no dependents, and as far as tax forms go, it's easy and quick to complete.

Getting Started:

1. Print out the 1040EZ form from **IRS.gov** or pick up a hard copy from your local library.

2. Fill out your tax form on paper first. You can submit via mail or online.

3. Visit **Vita-Volunteers.org** to get trained in how to do your taxes. You can also learn how to help others do theirs.

4. Visit a tax preparer to review your tax return. Ask them if you filled it out correctly or if they have any suggestions.

❐ 65. Read *Rich Dad, Poor Dad*

Very few people really know how money works or how to create wealth. Despite all of our education, most people are financially illiterate. As a result, we live in a debt-based economy instead of living debt-free lives.

For instance, you may want to buy a home someday. But is a house a liability or an asset? A house doesn't generate income for you unless it appreciates in value or it is used as a rental property. In the short term, a house can be a liability; it's really a long-term investment. Instead, if you buy an income property and rent it out, then you have an asset because it increases your income every month.

This is just one of the many mental shifts about money that you will gain from reading *Rich Dad, Poor Dad*. It shows you how rich people approach money with a different mindset than poor people, and thus the rich get richer. Though you are only a college student and may not have tons of money now, start to manage the little you have with the right mindset. This will make it easier for you to build wealth when your income increases over time.

Getting Started:

1. Buy *Rich Dad, Poor Dad* by Robert T. Kiyosaki at
   101Grads.com/Rich-Dad.

2. Read it and think of ways to apply its principles to your
   financial situation.

3. Invest in an asset within your current budget. This can be
   as small as buying a candy machine and putting it in a
   local store or as big as investing in a rental property.

❒ 66. Write A Business Plan

Once you take your last final exam and turn in your last paper you will transition into the business world. But unless you majored in business, accounting, or economics, you probably didn't learn the fundamentals of business. Anyone who understands business basics by graduation will have a leg up on anyone who doesn't.

Writing a business plan will teach you about business models and business language. A business model is how a company makes money. And just like a foreign language, business language will help you communicate and navigate the business world. Writing a business plan can also help you think critically about how you can use your passion to solve a problem for someone else. Most importantly, it will teach you the basics of business whether you're planning to be an entrepreneur or an employee. As you research companies for internships or full-time careers, thinking about a potential employer's business plan will give you a better idea of how to serve them.

The next time you and your friends come up with a money-making idea, try to write a business plan for the idea. Think about such factors as the market size, distribution channels, pricing, operations, cost structure, revenue model, company culture, sale strategy, product positioning, competitive advantage, and the financials. Successful business-plan writing will require at least average math and English, but it also requires creativity. Like the business world, this exercise will call on many aspects of your educational experience.

Getting Started:

1. Check out sample business plans at **101Grads.com/ Business-Plans**.

2. Write a business plan for a product or service idea you've always had that you think can make money. The point of this exercise is to help you explore ways you can turn your passion into a profit.

3. Compete in the business plan competitions compiled by *The New York Times* **101Grads.com/Business-Competitions** and search the web for "business plan competitions" as well.

☐ 67. Sell Something & Make A Profit

Though we buy products and services everyday, most people don't understand what goes into selling those products and services. Simply selling something on-campus as a fundraiser or for-profit venture will help you understand business basics such as revenues, expenses, profit, marketing, and sales.

Find some product or service that you can market and sell. Consider selling lemonade, roses for Valentine's Day, tickets for an event you organize **(SEE #85)**, or t-shirts about beating your school's rival. What do you need to do to attract customers? How do you price your items? What expenses do you have to factor in as "overhead?" Learn from the experience whether you make money or lose it.

Getting Started:

1. Set a S.M.A.R.T. goal **(SEE #87)** of trying to make $100 selling some sort of product in the next 30 days.

2. If it works, write a business plan **(SEE #66)** and try to grow the idea month-by-month.

3. Explore other college start-ups at **101Grads.com/College-Startups**.

❏ 68. Get Paid To Do What You Love

You've probably heard some variation on "Follow your passion and you'll find that money will come to you." It sounds nice, but there's more to getting paid for doing what you love than blindly following your passion. We all would love to spend all day working at something that doesn't feel like work—it would be like getting paid to have fun. However, most people don't have this opportunity not because it's not possible, but because they never took the time to see if their passion is worth something.

In order to turn your passion into something of monetary value, you have to figure out what marketable skills you have that can support your passion. For example, if you have a passion for travel, you have to go through the skills you possess that will help you fund your passion. If you have good writing skills, you can write articles about travel, ghost-write books for others on traveling, start a travel blog and sell advertisements, etc. If you are a good public speaker, you can be a tour guide or speak on cruise ships. If you have a knack for creating great videos, you can film your adventures. There are countless avenues that can allow you to pair your passion with your skills to make money.

Getting Started:

1. Draw a Venn Diagram and label one circle passions and the other circle skills.

2. Make a list of all of the things you love to do in the passions circle.

3. Using your skills list **(SEE #30)**, list your top 3-5 in the skills circle.

4. In the middle, identify career ideas that would allow you to combine your passions and skills.

5. Visit **Elance.com** and enter your skills and passions as keywords. See what opportunities come up.

6. Apply to 3 of the projects listed on **Elance.com**.

❐ 69. Interview 3 Professionals About Your Career Trajectory & Salary

One of the biggest mistakes college students make when thinking about their future job is expecting a high salary when they graduate.

Sure, you've read about some college grads getting $60,000 to $100,000 per year on their first job, but that's not always the case. In fact, expecting too high of a salary turns off potential employers for two reasons:

1. It makes them see you as arrogant.

2. It shows them you haven't researched what someone in your field receives for an entry-level position.

Don't let your expectations and lack of research hurt your candidacy. Salary research is never entirely accurate, but knowing a reasonable salary range is a good start.

The best way to find out more about what a career offers is by interviewing those who hold the jobs you want.

Getting Started:

1. Write down three careers you are interested in pursuing. The more specific the better.

2. Ask your career team **(SEE #57)** if they may know someone who has one of those careers.

3. If you cannot find someone, visit your career center or alumni center for support.

4. Take the time to conduct an informational interview **(SEE #49)** with a person who has the job you want.

5. Ask what a reasonable salary is for an entry-level position. Compare it to what you find on **Salary.com.**

6. Ask if there are any skills **(SEE #30)**, achievements, certifications **(SEE #32)**, or experiences that will help boost your entry-level salary.

7. Ask them about their career path and for any advice.

8. Follow up with a thank-you note **(SEE #81)**.

☐ 70. Get Your Real Estate License

You probably intend to own a home at some point in your life so you should learn about the home buying process beforehand. This will help you save money when you do decide to buy. College graduation is not a requirement to get your real estate license. You can find classes online for less than $300, the exams cost around $60, and the broker or salesperson license itself costs another $300. In total, that's less that $700 to learn the basics about one of the largest investments you'll ever make.

By getting your license now, you'll learn how to properly evaluate and value a home. This will help you avoid getting ripped off later, and you'll be able to take many of the middlemen out of the equation, which will save you far more than $700.

On top of that, you'll have another potential revenue stream after college. When your friends are ready to rent apartments or buy condos or homes, you can help them out for less than a broker or realtor would charge them. Apartment brokers usually charge fees of one month's rent. Realtors usually get 6% of the sales price. And real estate agents usually get 30-40% of what the realtor gets, which is 1.8-2.4%. An extra couple thousand dollars here and there will help out tremendously as you pursue your own financial goals.

Getting Started:

1. Research the real estate licensing process in your state.

2. Visit **RealEstateLicense.com** to learn how to get your license.

3. Take a course.

4. Take the exam.

5. Sell something!

MONEY, FAME, & BEAUTY ARE NOT THE ONLY WAYS TO MEASURE SUCCESS

Success

How do you define success? Although money, fame, status and power are commonly seen as measures of success, both the wisdom of the ages and today's best psychological research clearly show that real success comes from having a sense of purpose in our work, meaningful connections with the people around us, and a healthy balance in our lives. In and of itself, college has very little to do with helping you achieve this type of success. You have to take ownership of your life and create a college experience that will lay the foundation for a truly successful life.

There is a hidden curriculum that will help you be more successful, but you won't find it in most classrooms. What we've discovered is that the x-factor to success lies in knowing your **why**. The clearer you are on the reason, purpose, or intention behind your action, the more likely it is that you will succeed at it. When you know your **why**, you can tap into your intrinsic motivators, such as your passions, and this ends up giving you an edge over people only driven by extrinsic motivators like grades, prestige, or money.

When our parents' generation graduated from college the bar for success was a lot lower. All they had to do was outperform the people on their left or their right in high school and that would put them on a path where they could have a nice job, nice house, and nice kids like you. When we graduated from high school, we simply had to outperform the students in our state and we would be awarded admissions to some of the top public and private universities.

In his book *Success Built To Last*, Jerry Porras studied 200 of the world's most successful people including Lance Armstrong, Maya Angelou, Jeff Bezos, Sir Richard Branson, Bono, Michael Dell, Bill Gates, Phil Knight, Warren Buffet, and Bill Clinton, to name a few. One of his key findings is that highly successful people are driven to do what they love. They don't make major life choices to please others. Yet a lot of people spend their lives trying to satisfy everyone else's expectations and in the process, they end up hating themselves.

At the end of the day, success is striving to be the best you are and doing what really matters to you. Of course, in order to do what you love, you first have to figure out where your passions lie. For many students, this takes time—it's a journey of discovery, rather than a destination that's already known.

Exploring your career options, establishing a solid financial foundation, and taking advantage of all that college offers academically are important steps to take as you start your journey. But much can be learned by taking side trips along the way, to see whether your *why* lies in an unexpected direction. The items in our last chapter offer you opportunities to discover more about yourself and what motivates you. You may be surprised by some of these items, but don't dismiss them without trying them. If you do, you may never find your own personal passion, and you'll miss out on living your life to your full potential for success. And, in the long run, isn't that why you are in college?

❑ 71. Learn To Cook 5 New Dishes

If you are anything like how we were in college, most of the recipes you make include the following steps:

1. Place item in microwave.

2. Set timer.

3. Press start.

Eating only microwaved food is not a recipe for a successful life. It's not good for your health and it's not good for your quality of life. Having cold pizza for breakfast and cereal for dinner every day will run you down in more ways than one, and eating out all the time will make your wallet pretty thin.

Besides doing laundry, cooking is one of those life skills that you'll need to know no matter what you decide to do after college. Plus, being able to make good food always makes finding friends easier. You need 5 staple dishes that are quick and easy to make, so like Scarlett O'Hara, you can say, "As God is my witness, I'll never be hungry again!"

Getting Started:

1. Sign up for a cooking class on or off campus.

2. Ask friends who can cook to teach you a few simple meals.

3. Buy a basic cookbook, visit a cooking website for beginners or watch a cooking show.

4. Browse through the books and websites and find five easy and appealing dishes. You can find recipes for college students at **101Grads.com/Cooking**.

5. Purchase a basic cooking set and a few key ingredients such as olive oil, salt and pepper.

6. Practice until perfect and share with others by hosting a potluck **(SEE #77)**.

❏ 72. Play An Intramural Sport For Fun

Even though you're legally an adult, it's important not to forget the concept of play. Playing an intramural sport will keep you mentally competitive and physically healthy at the same time.

You've been competing since you were born. You may have had to apply to get into your high school, junior high school, or even elementary school. You competed against other college applicants on your SATs and admissions applications. And once you step into the business world, the competition only increases. Competition can be stressful, but we encourage you to find a healthy level of competition to push yourself. Playing intramural sports is one of the best ways to do that.

You may be out of shape after gaining the Freshman 15. After the age of 18, you'll start to realize that your body can't do everything it used to. It doesn't move as fast or heal as quickly, but intramural sports will whip you back into shape in a fun way that avoids treadmills and dumb bells. Pick any sport from basketball to racket ball to ultimate frisbee and have fun.

Getting Started:

1. Check out this list of sports at **101Grads.com/Sports**.

2. Go to your campus gym or fitness center to see if intramural sports are offered.

3. Buy or rent the necessary equipment and learn about the game and its rules.

4. Practice. Practice. Practice.

5. Join a team and have fun.

❏ 73. Get A Physical Exam Every Year

Good health is the foundation for everything, including a successful college career. This doesn't mean you have to run an Ironman Triathlon to get a 4.0 GPA, but being in good health helps. Can you imagine trying to pay attention in class if you feel sick all of time? What if you're too sick to even attend class?

Sure, you know to see a doctor if you are not feeling well or at least call home to ask your parents what to do, but not all illnesses have obvious symptoms. This isn't to make you nervous or turn you into a hypochondriac, but to make you aware that there's more going on with your body than you realize. It's important to get a complete physical exam and a clean bill of health from a doctor every year to ensure that your health isn't holding you back.

A complete physical exam includes measuring your height, weight, balance, reflexes, and eyesight, as well as blood and urine tests.

Getting Started:

1. If your parents have insurance, ask them which doctor you should see for a physical.

2. If you don't have insurance, visit your college's clinic or a local clinic to see how much a physical exam would cost. In most cases, the fee is low for students.

3. Set up an appointment for a physical exam.

4. Go through all of the test results with the doctor and ask for a copy that you can keep on file for your records.

❏ 74. Run A Marathon

Running a marathon is one of those things everyone should do once and there is no better time to do it than after you put on the Freshman 15. If you're like many people, you stopped engaging in athletic activities when you got to college, and it's amazing how quickly your health and fitness can start to deteriorate. First it's dorm to class, class to dorm, and then as soon as you graduate it becomes home to work, work to home. Most of your life is going to be spent sitting down unless you get up off your butt.

Running a marathon is just as much a mental challenge as it is physical. You will be pushed beyond what you consider your physical and mental limits. And it's not until you push yourself to your limits that you realize that you are limitless. With practice, you'll get rewarded by visible changes. Whether your legs get stronger or your time gets faster you will see yourself improve. Usually when there is evidence of physical growth, mental growth has also occurred.

Ultimately, your health is of utmost importance. No amount of education or money can counter high blood pressure or heart disease. Your time and your health are your two most valuable assets. You can't control everything that affects your overall health, but you should manage the things that you can such as your exercise and eating habits.

Getting Started:

1. Find a local marathon and sign up to run.

2. Train with a group for a few months.

3. Visit **MarathonGuide.com** for tips, tools, and resources on running marathons.

❏ 75. Abstain From Something For 30 Days

In Greek mythology, the story is told that Achilles' mother received a prophecy that her son would die in battle from an arrow in the foot. To protect him, she dipped him as a baby into a pool of invincibility but when doing so she held him by the heels. Sure enough he was later shot in the foot with an arrow and died from the wound. Today, having an Achilles' heel means having one weakness that leads to a downfall in spite of overall strength.

Most of us aren't oblivious to our Achilles' heel. We know what that one thing is that stops us from becoming who we truly want to be—procrastination, laziness, alcohol, low self-esteem, smoking, arrogance, entitlement, perfectionism, anger, over-eating, etc. Now imagine the huge positive difference in your life if you just stopped doing that one thing.

Try releasing your Achilles' heel for 30 days and observe the difference. We believe that when you do it, you'll want to continue for another month, a year, or even the rest of your life. Sometimes success in life isn't about adding stuff—instead it can be about clearing things away.

Getting Started:

1. Identify one thing that is detrimental to your success that you want to give up for 30 days.

2. Write down a list of behaviors that you need to change to let it go.

3. Also write down a list of things that might change for the better in your life if you let this thing go.

4. Journal **(SEE #95)** about your experience daily and/or create a "30 Day Do It" **(SEE #88)** goal around your Achilles' heel.

5. Visit **ExperienceProject.com** to read success stories of people who may be going through the same challenges as you.

❐ 76. Learn To Meditate

Meditation is no longer something that only Buddhist monks do. It's a go-to practice for many successful individuals.

If you have ever sought a way to get more clarity and focus in your hectic college life, meditation is the tool for you. It allows you to take a moment to calm your mind and refocus on what's important.

Learning to meditate doesn't require you to convert to a new religion—it is used by people of all faiths. And you don't have to spend hours trying to achieve Nirvana or silence your mind. It's not a race to get to a goal. Just try it for a couple of minutes. The more you practice meditation, the easier it will be to get into a calming state.

Getting Started:

1. Find a quiet, private place where you won't be disturbed for 10 to 20 minutes.

2. Turn off your cell phone and any other distractions.

3. Sit comfortably with your back straight, your eyes lowered, your face and hands relaxed.

4. Pay attention to your breath.

5. Count "One" on an inhale and then count "Two" on the exhale. Continue counting until you get to 10, and then start over again at "One."

6. Each time a new thought enters your mind, let it go without getting frustrated. Your mind is just doing its job. Return your breath and count.

❒ 77. Host A Potluck Dinner

Though college is a very social environment, most relationships tend to stay on the surface. What people really want is intimacy—deep relationships with people that allow them to feel connected. We don't just mean the romantic version of intimacy that bonds you and a significant other—we mean the intimacy that connects you and your friends as you go through life, from high school on.

Many of the social spaces in college don't allow for intimacy to be cultivated. It's too hard to have a real conversation with someone while screaming over music at a party or a club. The focus of sporting events is the teams at play, not the person sitting next to you. And **Facebook.com** definitely doesn't do the trick.

Food is a great way to bring people together, open them up, and help them connect. You've probably experienced this at holiday meals. But you don't have to wait until Thanksgiving to cultivate that space. Hosting a potluck dinner is an easy way to share food and food for thought with friends. It will allow you to have deeper conversations about life that can't happen as easily at a party, game, or another social event.

Getting Started:

1. Visit **101Grads.com/Potlucks** to learn more about potlucks.

2. Download the Potluck Starter Kit.

3. Open up your email account or **Evite.com**, choose your guest list, and send out an invitation to people you want to deepen your relationship with—male and female.

❏ 78. Interview Your Elders

With the Internet at our fingertips our generation thinks we know more than most adults. But there is a difference between having information and having wisdom. Our elders have a lot of untapped wisdom about life, love, happiness, success, family, and the world, and we can access it if we just ask.

Be grateful if you still have your grandparents in your life because not everyone does. Even if you don't, you can still cross this item off of your list by just talking to an elder you happen to know (e.g. parents, aunts, uncles, neighbors, etc). Some great questions to ask include:

- What's the greatest lesson life has taught you?
- Do you have any fears? How do you handle your fears?
- What did you want to be when you grew up? What happened?
- How do you define love? Success? Happiness? God? And how have those definitions changed over time?
- Do you have any regrets? Is there anything that you wish you would have done that you didn't?
- What was your toughest relationship? What lessons did you learn from it?
- What's your most memorable moment? Why?
- Tell me about your first _____ (kiss, job, flight, etc).

This experience will create more clarity and confusion in your life than you ever imagined. Some of your existing assumptions and beliefs will be challenged and some will be confirmed. Though times have changed, there are some fundamental truths about life that don't. Talk less and listen more on this one.

Getting Started:

1. Find one or two elders in your family or community, and ask them life's tough questions.

2. Hear what they have to say and capture it on video or audio.

3. Visit **101Grads.com/Elder-Interviews** for more great questions.

❑ 79. Go On A Road Trip Or Camping Trip

In college, most of your friendships will begin because of convenience. For instance, you have three classes with someone in one semester or you live near someone for a few years and now you're good friends. It's great how college can bring people together so naturally. You weren't looking for a best friend or a partner, but now you have one. However, relationships based on chance alone tend to fade when they are no longer convenient. One of the best ways to build lasting relationships is to do inconvenient things together by choice, like going camping or going on a road trip.

When two or more people willingly commit to doing something together, it says something about the relationship. You're all saying, "I want to be here with you now. You could be somewhere else with whomever, but you are choosing to be with me and I'm choosing to be with you—not by chance, but by choice."

When you're in the woods or on the road together, there will be conflicts, laughter, conversations, fights, hugs, stories, emotions, debates, and memories that will bond you together forever. The new situations and environments will cause you to test each other's boundaries and allow you to see who each other really is outside of the bubble of college. These new experiences together will serve as great opportunities to deepen your friendships and have fun.

Getting Started:

1. Choose three relationships that you value, but you know were born out of convenience, and organize an inconvenient yet fun activity to do together.

2. Visit **RoadTripAmerica.com** to plan a road trip, whether it's cross-country or shorter.

3. Check out the best camp grounds in the United States at **TripleBlaze.com** to organize a camping trip.

4. Be ready to fight, forgive, argue, agree, loathe, and love.

⧉ 80. Write A Letter Of Forgiveness

Growing up, you were probably taught to say "please" and "thank you", but were you taught to forgive? Forgiveness isn't as easy to do as saying "thank you," but it is equally important.

We all have been wronged in some way by others, but we have the choice to forgive. Walking around with the thoughts of anger, pain, and revenge is never helpful or healthy. We hang on to those feeling because we feel they are justified. But the secret that happy people discover is that those feelings hurt us far more than they punish anyone else.

You have to put yourself in the other person's shoes to begin to forgive. Have you ever done something wrong to another? After it happened, you may have apologized, but how did it feel when the other person didn't accept your apology? What you felt at that moment may be what your wrong-doer is feeling at this moment. Forgiveness is cathartic for you and for the other person.

Getting Started:

1. Think of someone who has hurt you.

2. Write a letter expressing how they hurt you and why you are forgiving them.

3. You can mail it to them or just keep it for yourself.

❐ 81. Write 5 Thank-You Notes

If you are like most people, the only time you wrote thank-you notes was after birthday parties when your Mom forced you to thank your Aunt Bea for that pea-green sweater that was two sizes too big.

That has to change. Though small, thank-you notes can have a big impact on your life.

Thank-you notes are key to making a great impression, establishing a professional relationship, and standing out from a crowd. Acts of gratitude are also important building blocks to a happy life.

Thank-you notes should follow every job interview, informational interview, referral, or favor that a contact does for you. A thank-you note expresses gratitude to your mentors and contacts for their help and guidance. Mentors look forward to hearing that their work has led to a positive outcome and that you've taken their advice.

Getting Started:

1. Buy a stack of blank thank-you cards from a card store. Make sure you buy cards that look professional.

2. Buy stamps.

3. Type up a first draft of your message on your computer to make sure there are no spelling or grammar mistakes. For ideas on what to write in your thank-you note, visit **101Grads.com/Thank-You-Notes**.

4. Write your message in pen. Do not type your thank-you note. You want it to be personal.

5. Send out your card within 48 hours of the meeting or event.

❐ 82. Volunteer For 30 Hours In A Semester

Volunteering has two major benefits—service and self-discovery. Volunteering is also a great way to discover your passion because it is driven by intrinsic motivators. With money, status, and recognition out of the equation, you get the opportunity to do what your heart naturally desires.

Whereas most paid jobs require you to climb your way up the corporate ladder to leadership, volunteer work can provide you with some of the best leadership opportunities possible. Whether you're building a home through Habit for Humanity, tutoring youth in the inner city, or spreading the word about an upcoming blood drive, you may be given a lot of responsibility quickly because the needs you are working for are very important and immediate.

30 hours in a 16 week semester isn't a lot—that's less than 2 hours per week. There are so many social problems like poverty, hunger, educational inequalities, and global warming that need talented minds addressing them because the for-profit market has yet to see the opportunity in solving these issues. In addition to serving as great work experience, it will give you a different perspective on life and a deeper appreciation for what you have.

Getting Started:

1. Identify a cause (e.g. poverty, genocide) or community
    (e.g. foster youth, the elderly) that you feel connected to.
    With volunteer work, it's essential that you really care
    about the issue or problem. Otherwise, you run the risk of
    dropping the ball, which is unfair to the cause you've
    signed on to help with.

2. See if your campus has a community service office and let
    them know the types of opportunities you are looking for.

3. Visit **VolunteerMatch.org**, **Sparked.com**, or
    CatchAFire.org to find volunteer opportunities near you.

❑ 83. Be A Mentor

Though you are still a student and have yet to learn a lot about life, in your 18-plus years on Earth you've already gained a lot of wisdom that you can share with others who want to be where you are. You can mentor underclassman, high school students, junior high school students, and your siblings or other family members and help them get where they want to go in life.

You don't have to have the wisdom of the Dalai Lama to be an effective mentor. The true foundation of mentorship is trust, which can only be garnered over time through your interactions and the way others see you live your life. Sometimes those around us just need an open ear and all you have to do is listen effectively. Mentoring isn't about giving others the right answer—it's about helping the mentee get a sense of all their options so that they can make the choice that is best for them.

Mentoring can be one of the most rewarding things you do if you commit to the success of those you are supporting as if it were your own. Give them the time, energy, support and resources to grow beyond your imagination and theirs!

Getting Started:

1. Identify your area of expertise (e.g. math skills, getting into college, public speaking) or an experience that you've overcome (e.g. first-generation student, foster care) that you think you can guide other willing people through.

2. Search your local community or the web for organizations that teach what you know or serve people who are going through what you've been through.

3. Check out Big Brother Big Sister (**BBBSA.org**) or visit **Mentoring.org** to find mentoring opportunities.

❒ 84. Raise $1,000 For A Cause You Care About

Knowing how to raise money for a problem, person, or project is a great skill to acquire whether you become an employee or an entrepreneur. This is your opportunity to test your storytelling ability to convince family and friends to contribute to something you really care about.

Once you determine the cause you are committed to supporting, the next step is getting informed and clarifying why this cause is personally important to you. Your ability to evoke emotion as you share why you got involved with this particular cause is what will move people to want to contribute to the cause through you.

The best way to move someone to action is through story. Storytelling is one of the most powerful skills you can graduate with. It's the ability to captivate the minds and hearts of those listening and take them on a journey with you to see what's possible for themselves. Storytelling combined with your ability to sell an idea, vision, product, service, program, or organization will be extremely valuable to you in the real world.

Getting Started:

1. Choose a cause you believe in.

2. Research the cause in depth so that you can speak powerfully about it.

3. Sharpen your story about why you chose this cause.

4. Set a fundraising or resource goal (e.g. $1,000, 10 computers, 100 volunteers) and a timeline and go for it.

5. Check out **AIDSWalk.net** or **DonorsChoose.org** or **KIva.org** to explore the different causes your efforts can support.

❏ 85. Organize A Huge Event

It's impressive to be elected president of an organization and host a few meetings throughout the year. It's much more impressive to test your leadership by organizing a huge event for an organization where you have to build a team, manage logistics, market the event, and deliver a memorable experience.

There are two ways to approach this challenge:

1. Consider the events that interest you on your campus or in your community. These could be social, political, charitable or educational. Join the planning committee for the upcoming school year.

2. Create an original event from scratch.

There are all kinds of things you can do using an organization's money, your money, or no money. Ideas include: conferences, concerts, banquets, keynote speeches, rallies, public displays, run-a-thons, phone-a-thons, dance-a-thons, fundraisers, fashion shows, talent shows, voter registration drives, parties, forums, panel discussions, flash mobs, career fairs, fun fairs, road trips, city tours, free hugs days, days of silence, etc. You'll discover how exciting it is to be a part of something bigger than yourself and to see how everything comes together on the day of the event. The challenges you face leading people, managing resources, and marketing will prepare you for success in the business world.

Getting Started:

1. Identify a cause or issue you believe in.

2. Decide what kind of event will best allow you to contribute to this cause.

3. Mobilize a team to plan the event and set a date.

4. Market the event.

5. Execute.

❐ 86. Define The 3 Ways You Measure Success

How do you define success? Everyone's definition of success is different, but until we define it for ourselves, we tend to adopt society's default dashboard of success—wealth, power, status, beauty, and fame. There is nothing wrong with any of these metrics. They are only wrong when they aren't yours.

Until now, G.P.A. has been the ultimate measure of success, but now it's time to come up with your own. There are hundreds and maybe even thousands of ways to measure success, so don't be restricted in your options. Is it happiness, money , love, power, celebrity, professional recognition, places visited, lives touched, businesses built, prizes won, books sold, number of grand-kids, number of lessons learned, or number of moments that take your breath away?

The list could go on and on and on. What's important is that you come up with your own list and prioritize it because the worst thing that can happen is that you become successful according to someone else's dashboard and not your own.

Getting Started:

1. List all of the ways you think success can be measured.

2. Prioritize the list according to how you measure success.

3. Select your top 5 and write 1-3 sentences about why you measure success in this way.

❏ 87. Set 3 S.M.A.R.T. Goals For The Year

To make progress toward achieving your goals, it's helpful to turn them into S.M.A.R.T. goals (Specific, Measurable, Attainable, Realistic, and Time-bound).

Let's say one of your goals is to go with your friends to San Diego for spring break. So, make it a S.M.A.R.T. goal.

Specific: A specific goal is, "I want to spend spring break in San Diego with three friends." A vague goal is, "I want to do something fun over spring break."

Measurable: You need $500 for your share of gas money for the round trip, hotel room cost, and food for the week. This is more concrete than, "I need money for the trip."

Attainable: It's October, so you have about five months to save for your trip in April. You'll need to save $100 per month, or $25 per week, to go on the trip. You are more likely to see results with this goal than if you say, "I'll save any money that's left over at the end of the month."

Realistic: You and your friends will drive the 1,000 miles in 15 hours, splitting driving time between the four of you. An unrealistic goal is more like, "We'll make the trip in a day."

Time-bound: You'll have 75% of the money saved by March, versus "I'll have the money soon."

Getting Started:

1. Make a list of three S.M.A.R.T. goals for this school year.

2. Use our S.M.A.R.T. template to plan out your goals **101Grads.com/SMART-Goals**.

3. Put your goals in a place where you will see them every day and share them with a few friends who will hold you accountable **(SEE #88)**.

❏ 88. Start A "30 Day Do It" Group

It's one thing to set S.M.A.R.T. goals **(SEE #87)**. It's another thing to set up an accountability system to ensure that you accomplish them. As much as we fight against accountability and structure, we need them to progress. After college, many people stop growing because they don't have the kind of structure in their lives that demands progress. There are no scheduled classes, coaches or professors forcing you to turn in your paper, train for that marathon, or report back on your global travels. Procrastination takes over.

The "30 Day Do It" is a movement with the mission of creating the world's largest and most effective goal-setting movement. The idea is to end the concept of New Year's Resolutions by introducing the idea of New Month Resolutions. The premise is that we should set goals every 30 days in small groups.

The way the group works is that when each person sets a goal, they also create a cost for themselves. For example, my goal may be to complete my website by the end of the month and my cost for myself is to pay everyone in the group $30 if I don't or wash everyone's car by hand. The moment you create a cost for yourself, the likelihood of you achieving your goal increases. It becomes a game of positive peer pressure with you and your friends, as you move forward in life together. Try it and accomplish more in a year than you ever have before.

Getting Started:

1. Go to **30DayDoIt.com** and download the Group Starter Kit.

2. Identify 5 friends who have your back **(SEE #24)**.

3. Invite them to join you for a 90-minute goal-setting meeting.

4. Follow the instructions in the Group Starter Kit and host your first group.

5. Continue meeting every 30 days for a year and track your monthly results.

❏ 89. Create A Vision Board

You can only measure success according to your pre-determined vision. Just because you've gotten far in life doesn't mean it's in the direction that you wanted to go. As the proverb goes, "A people without vision will perish." Most people journey through life blindly and without purpose. They let life happen to them instead of them happening to life. As a result, they end up living someone else's vision (e.g. parents or employer) instead of their own.

You can drive through life using tunnel vision, rear-view vision, or peripheral vision. Tunnel vision is one-track thinking; it's limiting and narrow-minded. You only can only see things happening one way or not at all. Rear-view vision is backwards. Imagine trying to drive with a huge rear-view mirror. There is a reason that the windshield is 20 times bigger than the rear-view mirror—we are supposed to go forward. Peripheral vision is open-minded. It takes into account your immediate surroundings, as well as what's on the horizon. It allows you to see possibilities that tunnel vision and rear-view vision cut off.

A vision board will help you stay focused on where you are and where you want to go, instead of getting lost in detours and distractions. Creating a vision board that consists of words and images that represent who you want to be, what you want to do, and what you want to have can serve as a helpful reminder to guide your daily actions. Even when you get caught up in passing moments in life like an argument with your boyfriend or girlfriend, a bad grade on a test, or a fender bender, your vision board will always be there to remind you of the bigger picture.

Getting Started:

1. Get a poster board, some old magazines, scissors, and a glue stick.

2. Flip through the magazines and look for words and images that reflect your vision of your life and goals, and cut them out.

3. Glue the words and images onto the poster board until it is full.

4. Once you are done, put the poster board up in a place where you will see it every day.

❏ 90. Take A Personal Development Course

In college you will major in and master certain subjects, but the most important thing to master in life is yourself. Unfortunately, there aren't too many classes on campus that will help you answer life's toughest questions like "Who am I?" or "What is my purpose?" so you have to find spaces off-campus to help you get those answers.

You may not have thought deeply about these things since you wrote your purpose statement for your college application, but that's just the beginning of the journey. There are personal development gurus out there who have created experiences to help you discover meaning in your life. One class with them could be worth more to you than your entire education. It's worth the investment.

Getting Started:

1. Check out **LandmarkEducation.com** or **FranklinCovey.com** or **EE.org** or **TonyRobbins.com**.

2. Save your money by learning ways to cut down the cost of personal development courses and events at **101Grads.com/Personal-Development-Saver**.

3. Register and take the course!

MASTER OF
SELF
IS THE MOST
IMPORTANT
MASTERS
YOU CAN EARN

❏ 91. Create A "101 List" For Your Life

Most people call it a "bucket list," but we call it your "101 List." It's basically a list of all of the cool things you want to do before you die. In the same way we've created a list of things for you to do in order to maximize your college experience, we want you to create your own list of things to do to ensure you get the most out of your life.

If you visit **43Things.com**, you can connect with a community of people who have similar goals as you and also get ideas for new ones. People want to do a lot of amazing things such as climb Mount Everest, go skydiving, see the Northern lights, visit multiple countries, and learn how to play the guitar. Whatever you choose, make sure that it's meaningful to you.

It may not seem like it now, but life is short and so many people leave this earth with regrets. Success is all about doing what you want with your life. Time is your most valuable resource and you get to choose how you spend it. At the end of the day you won't be able to blame your employer, school, or even your family for taking up all of your time. Live your life to the fullest by integrating the things you want to achieve into every day. Yes, life happens. But you have a lot of say in how it happens. The best way to predict the future is to create it.

Getting Started:

1. Download the 101 List Template at **101Grads.com/101-Template**.

2. Generate a list of all of the things you hope to accomplish before you die in column A of a Microsoft Excel spreadsheet.

3. In column B, give each one a priority level of 1, 2, or 3 with 1 being the highest priority.

4. Choose one of your highest priority items and take action to achieve it right now (e.g. register for a cooking class, research local skydiving options, or buy your plane ticket to Mount Everest). Some of your items may coincide with things on the 101 Grads List so you'll get to check them off twice.

5. Visit **43Things.com** to get more ideas if necessary.

❏ 92. Read *The Alchemist*

The Alchemist paints a vivid picture of the trials and tribulations of a young boy named Santiago as he seeks out his Personal Legend. He encounters love, loss, and lots of other things that you will face in your own life as you seek your purpose.

You are the author of your life. College is just one of many chapters that you get to write and live. Too many people let others dictate their life for them. We call them the 5 Ps— parents, partner, preachers, professors, and police. At the end of the day, you will be responsible for all of your choices and you won't be able to point fingers or say, "They made me do it."

Like Santiago you must develop the courage to ask yourself tough questions and then actively seek out the answers even if it means leaving your comfort zone.

Getting Started:

1. Buy *The Alchemist* at **101Grads.com/Alchemist**.

2. Your Personal Legend is your reason or purpose for living. Write a potential Personal Legend for yourself below:

Example: *My Personal Legend is to help people align their purpose and passions with a profession so that they can make a living doing what they love.*

_____

_____

_____

_____

_____

_____

_____

❏ 93. Read A Spiritual Text Cover To Cover

Many of us are born into religions and we only believe what we believe because our parents believed it. This is your opportunity to explore your beliefs now that you are away from your parents' influence.

Spirituality is the unseen core of our lives and it's easy to forget about it when you're in college. You may not have transportation to get to a house of worship. You may feel uncomfortable looking for a new place of worship. Or you may not even be interested in a relationship with a spiritual source right now.

When and if you ever feel curious, we encourage you to choose a spiritual text—the one you were raised on or one that just interests you—and read it from cover to cover. If nothing else, you will better understand a foundation text that has motivated countless lives. And you may end up find a connection to a spiritual tradition that will enrich your life. It may be the one your parents believe in and it may not be. Seek and ye shall find.

Getting Started:

1. Check out Amazon.com's Religion & Spirituality section to find a book that interests you. Visit **101Grads.com/ Spiritual-Books** and buy it.

2. Explore your relationship with your spiritual source as you read from the text regularly.

❒ 94. Visit Your Country Of Cultural Origin

Unless you're Native American, the United States is not your country of cultural origin. America is a land of immigrants and as ironic as this may be, the land of the free is made up of the descendants of persecuted people.

Native Americans, who were here first, were persecuted by the new settlers. Most Europeans came to America either because they were persecuted in their country of origin for their religious beliefs or because they were oppressed by poverty and social class. Africans were brought to America in slavery and continued to be persecuted long after Emancipation. Most of our ancestors withstood hardships that we can barely imagine.

The more you understand where your people came from and what they experienced, the more insights you'll have about your own life and your immediate family. You don't have to dig far back into the centuries, although that can be interesting. The Great Depression is still within living memory and it was a hugely important force in the lives of many families. Find out where your family was 25 or 50 or 75 years ago, and you'll start to see yourself as part of an ongoing story.

Getting Started:

1. Ask the oldest people in your family about your family history.

2. Find out when different parts of your family came to the United States and where they came from.

3. Do some outside research on your family name for leads and clues.

4. You can explore your family history with a saliva-based DNA test offered by National Geographic here **101Grads.com/DNA-Test**.

5. Book a plane ticket to your country of cultural origin and explore your history.

❑ 95. Journal For 30 Days In A Row

Socrates said: "An unexamined life is not worth living." Typically we only evaluate ourselves on New Year's Eve or our birthday. At those key moments we reflect back on who we were, who we've become, what we've accomplished, and what we hope for going forward. Journaling is one of the healthiest and cheapest self-discovery exercises you can do.

Imagine only being graded one time per year. We desire constant feedback because we like to know our progress. If you look yourself in the mirror each day, you can witness and make small changes to who you are the next day and the next day. Ultimately, you will develop a habit of self-evaluation through journaling your life daily, and one day you will arrive at a person and a place within yourself that you fall in love with.

Getting Started:

1. Buy any type of journal or notepad.

2. Set a daily or nightly alarm on your cell phone to remind you to write.

3. Free-write for 5-10 minutes non-stop using the prompt "Who was I today, and who do I want to be tomorrow?"

4. Continue this process for 30 days in a row.

❒ 96. Watch 20 Videos On TED.com

TED.com comes from the Technology, Entertainment, and Design conferences that draw thousands of amazing scientist, artists, entrepreneurs and designers together to share cutting-edge discoveries. The website has over 500 videos of world experts sharing their diverse passions. Most videos are 18 minutes long and extremely inspirational. **TED.com** is all about spreading astounding ideas. Watching the talks will expose you to career paths, industries, people, and ideas that you never considered, and open your mind to new possibilities.

There are books that you will read during college that are timeless. But for the most part, your textbooks can't keep up with the speed of the world. The moment it is published, a textbook is outdated—that's why you have the 5th, 6th, and 7th editions. Talks on **TED.com** are current and they envision the future. They can help you stay on the cutting-edge of developments related to your industry and the world.

You sit in 60 to 90 minute lectures every day that move slower than your mind. In 18 minutes, a TED Talk will expand your mind as you absorb the insights, discoveries and forecasts of the world's most exciting doers and thinkers. Old knowledge like Pythagoras' theorem is important to understand, but you also want to ensure that you add a healthy dose of new knowledge to your mental diet because the best ideas come from the merging of the known and the unknown.

Getting Started:

1. Go to **TED.com** and click on a theme that interests you or conduct a search for something you're interested in.

2. Find a video with a subject line that speaks to you and watch it.

3. Watch all 20 in an 8 hour day or spread them out over time.

4. Write a comment or a blog post about your thoughts on the videos you watched.

5. Share the videos on your online social networks.

❒ 97. Wear A Costume To Class

"Everybody is somebody, but nobody wants to be themselves."
- Gnarls Barkley, "Who Cares" from St. Elsewhere

When we were kids, we would say, "I want to be just like so-and-so when I grow up." Today, many of us still try to be like someone else—or like anyone other than ourselves. But no matter how hard we try, we can never succeed at being someone else. The easiest thing for you to be is you. Success is about discovering who you are and finding a space where being who you are is rewarded.

The primary reason we conform is because we want to be loved and accepted by others. To be loved and accepted is a beautiful thing unless you lose yourself in the process of trying to please everyone else. People-pleasers are successful in everyone's eyes except their own.

Wearing a costume to class on a day that's not Halloween will push you out of your comfort zone and help you address your fear of standing out and being different. That's exactly what successful people do—they are willing to stand out because they are different and they embrace it.

When you wear a costume, people will laugh at you, point at you, look at you funny, and question you. But once you've gone to the extreme of wearing a costume, you will feel more comfortable in your own skin afterward.

Getting Started:

1. Ask a friend if you can borrow their Halloween costume from last year or create a costume of your own. Avoid wearing a mask because it can be seen as threatening and it takes away from the experience of people knowing it's you.

2. Choose the day you're going to wear your costume to class.

3. Get dressed and go to campus just the way you would any other day.

4. Feel your emotions. Question your emotions. Laugh at your emotions.

5. Overcome your fear of standing out and being you!

❑ 98. Take An Alternative Spring Break

You can waste Spring Break or you can work Spring Break. It's up to you. There are so many amazing things you can do with a week of time if you plan ahead. These can include volunteering in another country, shadowing an alum on the job, completing a creative project you've been procrastinating on, or taking an off-campus class in something you want to learn. All of these activities will be more valuable to you in the short and long-run than going wild at MTV Spring Break in Cancun or vegging out watching MTV Spring Break on the couch at your parents' house.

You're probably burnt out from a tough semester, but that's why you need to do something that will give you new experiences and a fresh sense of possibilities. Planning something positive and exciting will give you something to look forward to as February and March drag by. You will get a boost of energy when you return, which will help you through April and May. Decide what you want to do and start planning in January and February.

Instead of going on vacation, do something that will advance your vocation.

Getting Started:

1. Decide on one thing you want to learn or experience during Spring Break.

2. Do research and garner the resources (e.g. money, supplies, space) and people (e.g. friends, alumni) needed to make it happen.

3. Visit **AlternativeBreaks.org** or **Encountour.com** to check out more alternative spring break ideas.

❏ 99. Sing Karaoke

Many of us are afraid of our own voices. That's why we don't raise our hands in class when we know the right answer or speak up when we have questions **(SEE #7)**. We're afraid of being wrong or of what others will think of us. Yet your input is valuable; it could provide the insight that changes the trajectory of the conversation. If you don't have the courage to raise your voice, then everyone stays stuck in their own old thoughts.

Karaoke will liberate you from the fear of your own voice. It will free you from worrying about what others think of you when you're being yourself. Karaoke is beautiful for two reasons:

1. There is no right way to do it. The more you mess up and the worse you sound, the more fun it actually is.

2. You can do it in a safe space with a group of friends if it's strangers that worry you, or you can do it with complete strangers if it's your friends' opinions that you're afraid of.

Once you've sung karaoke and made a complete fool of yourself in front of your friends and/or strangers, you will feel a greater sense of freedom to be yourself. You'll stop taking other people's opinions so seriously. You'll be more comfortable being who you are, no matter what. And there is no better way to live.

Getting Started:

1. Choose a night to sing karaoke with friends or strangers.

2. Practice your favorite pop songs in the shower or the car.

3. Go to the karaoke bar and sing your heart out.

❏ 100. Do Something You'll Likely Get Rejected From Or Fail At

Most people think that success means never failing, which is not true. If you can't tell a story about a personal failure, then you likely haven't reached the level of success you're capable of. Instead, you're stuck at a level that is merely comfortable and you haven't really pushed yourself. The world's most successful people have failed more than those who are less successful. They kept trying new ideas and iterations of old ones until they succeeded.

How come you haven't walked up to that hot guy or hot girl you've been drooling over since day one of the semester and just said hello? What makes you any less of a scholar than those who apply and become Rhodes Scholars or Fulbright Scholars? We challenge you to push yourself and that means exploring an area of uncertainty where you don't know if you're going to win or lose.

Run for office. Take an honors course that's above you. Try out for the football team even though you weren't recruited. Run a marathon **(SEE #74)**. Dare to be great—greatness is a choice about effort, not results.

Getting Started:

1. Identify a challenge that you're afraid of or that you think is just way out of your league.

2. Create a timeline to complete and/or prepare for the challenge.

3. Go for it with all of your heart, mind, and soul.

4. Regardless of what happens, rejoice in knowing that you tried your best to do something you thought was impossible for you to do.

❑ 101. Create Your Own List Item

The *101 Things To Do Before You Graduate* list will constantly evolve. As you change, as college changes, as the world changes, and as we change, the list will be updated with whatever is most relevant to college students' success in school and in life at the time.

We would love for you to add ideas to the list that have been important to your success or things that you intend to do that you think would enrich anyone's college experience.

Getting Started:

1. Visit **101Grads.com/Add** and share an item that you think should be added to the list.

NOTE: We will consider your submission and may write a blog post celebrating you and your contribution.

Afterword

Most college students are not prepared for the road from college to career. At some point while they were growing up they were told, "Go to a good college and you'll get a good job," and "Follow your passion and you'll be happy," and "Do what makes you happy," and "Go to graduate school and you can figure out your career direction there," and even "Don't major in that because you'll never get a job," among other completely misguided *words of wisdom*. As a result, most students don't have a clue about what to do during their college years other than go to class and have fun. So rather than wisely investing their most precious resource — time — they waste time on things that won't pay dividends in the future.

In addition, most college students expect the road to be straight, smooth, carefree and full of attractive choices— perhaps something like the Garden of Eden. But we all know that the world of work in the 21st century isn't like that at all. It is dynamic, global and extremely competitive. No matter what college you attended, nothing comes easy and nothing simply drops on your lap.

Rather than preparing ourselves for a single perfect job or career path, we must develop the mindset, knowledge and skills to thrive in this new world of work. By doing so, not only will we be able to identify and secure a decent job or graduate school spot, but we will be prepared to identify and secure the 10 or more different jobs we're likely to have throughout our lives.

If you finished reading *101 Things To Do Before You Graduate* and completed all the action items, congratulations! You have built a sound foundation for success in the 21st century. You have made the courageous decision to take control of your uncertain future. You have invested wisely in your personal capital, intellectual capital, social capital and financial capital. Keep these concepts in mind and continue to invest throughout your life. By doing so you will experience exponential growth and success beyond anything you can now imagine.

If you decided to read the Afterword before actually reading the core content and advice inside, that's OK too. But now read *101 Things To Do Before You Graduate* and complete the action items. Getting ahead in your career and life depend on you taking actions like these.

Colleges and universities have all the best intentions: part of their mission is to help you discover yourself, define your strengths and passions, and get you equipped for life after college. However, very few have the resources, programs or culture to help every student in a holistic way. Students are rarely required to do the type of soul searching, career and life exploration, job/career search preparation, or on-the-job/grad school performance readiness that's presented in this book.

No one expects students to have the ability to figure out all the correct steps and know exactly what's most important or even how to get started. That's why *101 Things To Do Before You Graduate* is the perfect resource for you. It's your guide to doing all the things that will best prepare you for life and career after college. As my good friend, Jullien Gordon would say, "Start your engines! It's time to get your vehicle moving on the amazing journey you were meant to live." The roadmap is right here in your hands.

I wish you many blessings on your journey from college to career.

Andy Chan
Vice President for Career Development
Professor of Practice – Schools of Business
Wake Forest University

Patricia Hudak is the founder and CEO of Real World 101. Patricia launched Real World 101 after graduating from college and finding herself with more questions than answers. She created Real World 101 as a resource she would have liked to have to smooth the transition from college to the rest of her life.

She is a graduate of New York University with Bachelors' degrees in Marketing and Management from the Leonard N. Stern School of Business.

ABOUT REAL WORLD 101

Real World 101 prepares college students and recent graduates for life after college.

Through our products and services, we successfully enable students to transition from college to the "real world" feeling more informed and confident.

We aim to make life less complicated for twenty-somethings everywhere.

Jullien Gordon is the son of two doctors. As a result, people expected him to be some sort of super-doctor. Instead, he became a superhero who goes by the name The PurposeFinder. As CEO of the Department of Motivated Vehicles, he spends his life helping individuals and organizations discover their purpose within and then helps them create business models that allow them to make a living doing what they love. Some people call it coaching and consulting, but Jullien calls it helping people D.R.E.A.M. awake. According to Jullien, to D.R.E.A.M. means to have your Desired Relationships Employment And Money, and success is the equilibrium of these three elements for each individual.

He is also passionate about writing. In addition to *101 Things To Do Before You Graduate*, he has published two other books titled—*The 8 Cylinders of Success: How To Align your Personal and Professional Purpose* and *Good Excuse Goals: How to End Procrastination & Perfectionism Forever*. Jullien blogs regularly at JullienGordon.com on, purpose, passions, personal growth and professional development.

In 2007, Jullien received two Masters degrees from Stanford University—his MBA and Masters in Education—and in 2003 he received his B.A. from UCLA in 3 years. Jullien Gordon is originally from Oakland, California and currently resides in Brooklyn, New York.

Real World 101 **Care Packages**

Do you have everything you need for the real world?

Sure, a diploma's nice, but can it help you do your taxes??

Real World 101 Care Packages contain all the information a college graduate needs to know to be prepared for life after college. It's what every college gradate should have if they want to succeed.

What's Inside?
- 3 Real World 101 Guide Books
- Free 3-Month Subscription to Real World 101 Online
- Real World 101 Multimedia Tools CD
- "Real World" Acceptance Certificate
- Real World 101 "I'm Ready for the Real World" T-Shirt
- Real World 101 Care Package Bag

RealWorld101.org/Care-Package-Program